Also by Phyllis Schlafly

A Choice Not An Echo (1964)
The Gravediggers (1964)
Strike from Space (1965)
Safe Not Sorry (1967)
The Betrayers (1968)
Mindszenty the Man (1972)
Kissinger on the Couch (1975)
Ambush at Vladivostok (1976)
The Power of the Positive Woman (1977)
The Power of the Christian Woman (1981)
Equal Pay for UNequal Work (1984)
Child Abuse in the Classroom (1984, rev. 1985, rev. 1993)
Pornography's Victims (1987)
Who Will Rock the Cradle? (1989)
Stronger Families or Bigger Government? (1990)
Meddlesome Mandate (1991)
First Reader (1994)
Allegiance (2000)
Turbo Reader (2001)
Feminist Fantasies (2003)
The Supremacists (2004, rev 2006)
The Flipside of Feminism: What Conservative Women Know—And Men Can't Say (2011)
No Higher Power: Obama's War on Religious Freedom (2012)

A CHOICE NOT AN ECHO

A
CHOICE
NOT AN
ECHO

PHYLLIS
SCHLAFLY

First edition, May 1964: 600,000 copies
Second edition, June 1964: 1,000,000 copies
Third edition, August 1964: 1,600,000 copies

The first edition of *A Choice Not an Echo*, published May 1, 1964, correctly
predicted who would be the kingmakers' candidates at the 1964 Republican
National Convention, and foretold the tactics they would use in their efforts
to stop Barry Goldwater. The third edition continued the history through the
1964 Republican National Convention in San Francisco that nominated Barry
Goldwater.

Regnery® is a registered trademark of Salem Communications Holding
Corporation.

Library of Congress Control Number: 2014945281

ISBN 978-1-62157-315-9

Published in the United States by
Regnery Publishing
A Salem Communications Company
300 New Jersey Ave NW
Washington, DC 20001
www.Regnery.com

Manufactured in the United States of America

10 9 8 7 6 5 4 3 2

Books are available in quantity for promotional or premium use. For information on discounts and terms, please visit our website: www.Regnery.com.

Distributed to the trade by
Perseus Distribution
250 West 57th Street
New York, NY 10107

Contents

— PART II —
The Battle Continues: 1968–2016

Foreword

by Dr. Ron Paul

It is a pleasure to write the foreword to the new edition of Phyllis Schlafly's *A Choice Not an Echo*. During my years in Congress, my staff worked closely with Phyllis's Eagle Forum on restoring parental control of education, protecting American sovereignty, and protecting privacy.

Phyllis was one of the few conservative leaders who endorsed my campaign to return to Congress in 1996. Her support was very helpful in overcoming the Republican Establishment's smear campaign designed to convince Republican primary voters that my consistent support of the Constitution and individual liberty somehow meant I was not a "real" Republican.

A Choice Not an Echo's account of how a small group of powerful kingmakers stole the Republican presidential nominations of the 1940s and 1950s will resonate with grassroots activists who today are fighting similar battles with the Republican Establishment.

As I saw in my presidential campaigns of 2008 and 2012—especially the latter—the Washington-based Establishment and the special interests that benefit from the welfare-warfare state still possess disproportionate influence over the two major parties as well as the mainstream media. These kingmakers use their influence in the presidential nominating process to ensure that the nomination is never captured by a candidate whose platform challenges the bipartisan support of the welfare-warfare state. Many of the younger activists who participated in my campaign will find a disturbing similarity between the Establishment's treatment of grassroots conservatives in the 1950s and 1960s and its treatment of the liberty movement in 2008 and 2012.

Of course, there have been some significant changes in American politics and the nomination process since Phyllis first penned this book. Since Barry Goldwater's campaign, the conservative movement has grown in size and influence within the Republican Party and in the country as a whole. As a result, the Republican Establishment has taken an "if you can't beat 'em, co-opt 'em" approach to conservatives. Some conservatives have found a quite comfortable place within the Establishment. These "conservatives" happily do the kingmakers' bidding by misleading the movement's foot soldiers into confusing the success of the conservative movement with the fortunes of the Republican Party.

The biggest change in the nominating process since this book was first published is that political parties no longer choose their nominees at conventions. Today conventions are week-long infomercials. The actual selection of presidential candidates is done through state primaries and caucuses. This system has both advantages and disadvantages for grassroots candidates challenging the Establishment's anointed candidates.

The primary system provides advantages to the candidate who can raise big money early, as well as receive media attention and big-name endorsements. Such candidates are usually those anointed by the kingmakers, but an outsider can, if backed with sufficient grassroots enthusiasm, upset the kingmaker-anointed candidate. This is especially the case in the Iowa caucuses and the New Hampshire primary, as grassroots organizing and person-to-person campaigning is still the key to winning in those states.

Another major change that benefits those challenging the Establishment is the rise of the internet and alternative news sources. When Phyllis wrote her 1964 book, most Americans got their news from one of three television networks, local newspapers whose national news was pulled from a wire service, or one or two major weekly news magazines. It was easy for the media to marginalize a candidate whose ideas were not approved by the Establishment. Today, a candidate "blacked out" by the mainstream media can still spread a message far and wide through the internet.

The use of YouTube, Meetup, Facebook, and other internet sites by my supporters is one reason why I was able to overcome the hostility of the GOP kingmakers, as well as blatant media bias, in 2008 and 2012. While I did not succeeded in getting the nomination, my campaign launched a grassroots movement (or "rEVOLution") that, much to the kingmakers' annoyance, is reshaping the Republican Party and American political and intellectual discourse.

Anyone who doubts that the mainstream media ignore, and then try to discredit, a candidate whose ideas they consider "out of the mainstream" should examine how they covered my campaigns. In 2008, the excuse that "Polls show Ron Paul cannot win so why should we treat him as a top-tier candidate?" may have had some justification. However, by the start of the 2012 campaign polls consistently placed me in the top tier, and I had one of the strongest and most loyal bases of support of any candidate. Yet the media continued to subject my campaign to biased coverage designed to discredit me, my followers, and my ideas.

In August 2011, I finished a close second in the influential Iowa straw poll. The media refused to acknowledge the result; one paper's headline even named the first and third place winners but conspicuously failed to mention the second place finisher. The few media outlets that did report on the straw poll results insisted on referring to me as "Ron Paul, who has no chance of winning the nomination." So, months before the first votes were cast, the mainstream media had already decided that I could not get the nomination, even though my campaign was rising in the polls and I came within a hair of wining the Iowa straw poll.

This scenario was repeated through the fall of 2011. Not only did the media do their best to ignore my campaign, but in debates I was consistently given less time than candidates who were trailing me in every major poll.

When the mainstream media finally acknowledged my candidacy, they began to ask me if I had any plans to run as third-party or independent candidate if I did not win the GOP nomination. The effect was to suggest to many Republican primary voters that I was not a "real" Republican. I never expressed any interest in running as anything but a Republican at any point during my 2012 campaign.

The media's hostility was matched by the reaction of Establishment Republicans. As the Iowa caucus got nearer and my campaign climbed higher in the polls, members of the GOP Establishment launched attacks on my campaign. The governor of Iowa, in a not so subtle attempt to discourage my supporters, warned that a Ron Paul victory would "discredit" the Iowa caucus.

Despite this clear attempt by the media and the Establishment to crush my candidacy, my campaign for liberty accomplished a stronger showing than any political expert had predicted. This was because both my official campaign and my grassroots supporters had mastered effective use of the internet to organize and spread the message.

One feature of my campaign that confused the media was the support I received from young people—more than any other Republican candidate. The reason had to do with the power of the ideas of liberty. My call for returning government to constitutional limitations, including a return to the Founders' foreign policy of "peace, commerce, and honest friendship with all, entangling alliances with none," and sound money resonated with young people who recognized that they are getting a bad deal from the current system.

Even after it became clear that I was not going to receive the nomination, my events attracted large crowds, especially at college campuses. In the spring of 2012, it was common for crowds of several thousand college students to come to my events. These crowds were not just at conservative colleges; one of our larger events, drawing over five thousand, was at Berkeley, California.

While thousands of young people were turning out to hear my message, the GOP Establishment was engaging in a campaign to slam the door in the face of these new voters. My campaign had organized my supporters to attend state GOP conventions and caucuses and get selected as delegates to the national convention in Tampa, Florida. For the most part, my supporters followed party rules. The Establishment did not respond in kind. Instead they broke their own rules, harassed my supporters—to the point of physically attacking them.

In Tampa, the Establishment increased its shabby treatment of the liberty movement. Delegates who were legitimately selected under the rules of their state were suddenly denied credentials for no other reason than that they were part of that "liberty" crowd.

The most outrageous activity of the convention was the changes in rules governing the future nomination process that were rammed through by the party leadership over the objections of the grassroots. These rules centralized and shortened the nomination and delegation selection process. The clear purpose of these rules is to advantage candidates who can raise big money early, which means candidates favored by the Establishment. The rules would even ensure that delegates to future conventions would be approved by the party nominee! It was not only my supporters who objected but also grassroots conservatives across the board and several prominent leaders, including Phyllis. Rush Limbaugh spent an hour denouncing the power grab on his radio show.

Despite the clear anger across the board, the Establishment went ahead with the rules change. In an infamous moment captured on YouTube, House Speaker Boehner, who was presiding at the convention that day, read from a pre-loaded teleprompter that "the ayes" had it and gaveled approval of the rules. Anyone on the floor—or who watches the video—can clearly see and hear that it is not clear that the "ayes" had it.

Observers might wonder why the Establishment would be so determined to block grassroots activists that they would alienate a substantial part of the party's base right before a presidential election? It was the same suicidal behavior that Phyllis described in *A Choice Not an Echo*: the upper echelon of the GOP is still controlled by an Establishment that would rather lose with a candidate who says "me too" to the bipartisan consensus than win with a candidate who challenges that consensus.

The large "McMansions" that litter the landscape in Northern Virginia provide physical evidence of how many in the political class benefit from the current system. Many of these houses are owned by lobbyists and other employees of the military-industrial and security-industrial complex. The influential occupants of these villas do not want a debate about foreign policy.

Other kingmakers want to block a debate about our financial system and monetary policy. They resent grassroots opposition to organizations such as the International Monetary Fund and the Export-Import Bank, which funnel American taxpayers' money to multinational companies. The kingmakers want an agenda free of any discussion of how Federal Reserve policies benefit big-spending politicians, big banks, Wall Street firms, and the international financial elites. If the American people learned the full truth about how the monetary system benefits these interests, there would be a political earthquake. This is why it is has been so difficult to pass the "Audit the Fed" bill, even though 75 percent of Americans support it.

Despite their continued ill-treatment by the GOP Establishment, the young liberty activists who flooded into the Republican Party in recent years are not going away. Despite the hope of the Establishment that the liberty movement would die out after I left Congress, its ranks are still growing.

These young people can benefit from reading how previous generations faced many of the same problems and overcame the kingmakers to nominate a grassroots candidate. They did it with Barry Goldwater in 1964 and with Ronald Reagan in 1980. We can do it again and offer the American people *A Choice Not an Echo*.

Part I

A Choice Not an Echo
1936–1964

1

The Billion Dollar Robberies

Newspapers still headline stories about the $7 million London train robbery of 1963 and the earlier $1.2 million Brink's robbery in 1950 in Boston. Yet the press is strangely silent about the $13 billion robbery of 1940, the $98 billion robbery of 1944, the $39 billion robbery of 1948, or the $81 billion robbery of 1960.

In each of those years the American people were robbed of their constitutional birthright to a presidential choice. At stake was control of the annual federal spending which rose from $13 billion in 1941 to $100 billion in 1964.

The advance planning and sense stimuli employed to capture a $10 million cigarette or soap market are nothing compared to the brainwashing and propaganda blitzes used to insure control of the largest cash market in the world: the executive branch of the United States government.

Most Americans think the next president of the United States will be selected on the first Tuesday after the first Monday in November 1964 when we go to the polls to vote. Most Americans think they will vote for a candidate who has been selected in their party's political convention by delegates who voted their honest convictions and chose the man best qualified to lead their party to victory. This may be what is taught in the schoolbooks, but this ideal is frequently contrary to political reality.

From 1936 through 1960 the Republican presidential nominee was selected by a small group of secret kingmakers who are the most powerful opinion makers in the world. They dictated the choice of the Republican presidential nominee just as completely as the Paris dressmakers control the length of women's skirts. In the 1940s when the decree went out from Paris that all women's skirts should be only fourteen inches off the floor, every family budget in the United States was unbalanced in a frantic effort to achieve the "new look."

Each fall sixty-six million American women don't spontaneously decide their dresses should be an inch or two shorter, or longer, than last year. Like sheep, they bow to the wishes of a select clique of couturiers whom they have never seen, and whose names they may not even know.

It is easy to predict that, when skirts get about as short as they can possibly go, a Paris edict will be handed down again, and otherwise-sensible American women, even when they cannot afford such extravagance, will throw or give away perfectly good dresses in order to buy new ones which will meet the fashion dictates of a half dozen dressmakers in Paris.

In the same way, a few secret kingmakers based in New York selected every Republican presidential nominee from 1936 through 1960, and successfully forced their choice on a free country where there are more than thirty-four million Republican voters. Fantastic? In this book, we will examine the record and see how they did it. The strategy of politics, like an iceberg, is eight-ninths under the surface.

But, first, let us look at the issues of the 1964 election year.

2

Who's Looney Now?

Every newspaper, every newscast on radio and television, every statement of public officials testifies to the numerous important political issues of the 1964 campaign year.

I. *Defeats around the world*. A map of the world reveals the collapse of American foreign policy everywhere.

Laos, as a result of the troika coalition government forced upon our friends by Ambassador Averell Harriman, is now under communist control. This is in spite of the fact that Laos received more United States foreign aid per capita than any nation in the world, and was the scene of the dedicated private charity of the heroic Dr. Tom Dooley.

Vietnam, slipping fast into Communist clutches, is now embroiled in a bloody war in which American boys are fighting and dying with little hope, under the policies of the present administration, of winning.

Cambodia, which has received generous amounts of foreign aid, has ordered our diplomatic representatives out of the country.

Pakistan and *India* are angry at us for the military aid we have given the other.

Greece, the country we saved from communism under the Greek-Turkish Aid Program, has been the scene of rampaging anti-American mobs which burn President Johnson in effigy.

France and *England*, our old friends, have broken with American policy, recognized Red China, and told President Johnson they will trade with Cuba and the Soviet Union whether we like it or not.

We have lost the friendship of our NATO ally *Portugal* because our State Department sided with Portugal's enemies when they seized Goa and attempted to seize Angola.

We have lost the friendship of our NATO ally the *Netherlands* because the Democratic policy under Bobby Kennedy encouraged Sukarno to steal Dutch New Guinea.

The *Congo*, as a direct result of the coalition policy forced upon it by the Democratic State Department through the UN, is in utter chaos, with gangs of savages terrorizing and killing missionaries and other white people.

In *Algeria*, communist Ben Bella, who was welcomed to America by the Democratic Administration with a 21-gun salute on the White House lawn, is building a Castro-like state.

In 1960 the Democratic presidential and vice presidential candidates made a major issue of our "image" abroad. They promised to increase respect for America among foreign countries. Four years later, Americans are more hated by more people than ever in our history. In many countries on every continent, the American flag is being dragged down, American property is being confiscated, American citizens are being seized and humiliated.

II. *Castro and Cuba.* After the Bay of Pigs invasion that turned into a triumph for Castro, and after the phony "blockade" of October 1962 that turned into a triumph for Khrushchev, the problem of Cuba is still with us. The Johnson administration apparently has no plans for doing anything to solve it. No one knows how many Soviet missiles are still in Cuba, aimed at targets in the United States. No one knows how many Soviet troops and "technicians" are directing military operations in Cuba and training Latin Americans for subversion.

We do have documented evidence that Castro is a fountainhead for subversion in Panama, Venezuela, throughout Latin America, and all the way to Zanzibar.

On January 17, 1964, Khrushchev repeated his claim that he had moved missiles out of Cuba only in return for a United States pledge not to invade that island. He said:

> We got a pledge that there will be no invasion of Cuba.[1]

Not a single responsible official of the Johnson Administration denied Khrushchev's boast. The American people can only conclude that the Democrats in fact did make such a pledge, and that the Johnson administration intends to fulfill it. Worse, the Democrats not only pledged no invasion of Cuba by the United States, but they are using our Navy and Coast Guard to prevent the Cuban Freedom Fighters from conducting guerrilla warfare against Castro.

The slogan of the Johnson administration seems to be:

> Don't worry about the Reds—they are
> still 90 miles away!

How long can we tolerate this communist base in Cuba, with Castro insulting and harassing us, spreading his infection throughout the Western

Hemisphere giving the Soviets the opportunity to zero in their missiles on American cities?

III. *Survival.* Hitler told the world his plans for world conquest in *Mein Kampf.* Western leaders refused either to read or to believe his clear design for aggression. The Communists also have laid out their blueprint for world conquest.

On November 18, 1956, Khrushchev told Western diplomats at a Moscow reception:

> Whether you like it or not, history is on our side. We will bury you.[2]

Each year Khrushchev has accelerated his timetable. On July 6, 1960 in Kaprun, Austria, he said:

> In the short time I still have to live, I would like to see the day when the Communist flag flies over the whole world.[3]

On January 17, 1961, Khrushchev predicted that the "victory of world Communism is no longer far off."[4] In Bucharest, Romania on July 19, 1962, Khrushchev boasted:

> I am convinced that tomorrow the Red flag will fly over the United States. But,

we will not fly the flag. The American
people will hoist it themselves.[5]

Khrushchev has tested and exploded super
hydrogen bombs many megatons more powerful
than ours. Communism controls one-fourth of the
earth's land surface and one-third of its population. In the last three years, our enemy has acquired
missile and submarine bases in Africa and in the
Western Hemisphere.

The most important national problem is the survival of American freedom and independence in the
face of the communist threat. Instead of promising
to protect our Republic from the greatest threat
in our history, the response of the present Democratic administration is summed up in three policy
documents:

1) *State Department Publication* 7277 entitled
"Freedom From War," which lays out the official
policy of the present administration to abolish our
Army, our Navy, our Air Force and our nuclear
weapons, and make us subject to a "United Nations
Peace Force."[6]

2) *The Rostow Report,* a master plan on foreign
policy and disarmament authored by Walt W. Rostow, chairman of the State Department's Policy
Planning Board.[7] The thesis of the Rostow Report
is that the communists are "mellowing," that we

must abandon our first-strike weapons, that we must not seek victory of the United States over the Soviet Union or of capitalism over communism, that we must never give any encouragement to revolts behind the Iron Curtain, that we should deny U.S. foreign aid to countries in order to force them into coalition governments with the communists as was done in Laos, that we must work toward general and complete disarmament, and that the administration should embark on a systematic publicity campaign in order to sell Congress and the American people on disarmament. These are now the policies of the Johnson administration.

3) *The Phoenix Report,* prepared for the U.S. Arms Control and Disarmament Agency.[8] The thesis of the Phoenix Report is that we should abandon the old objectives of "containment" and "coexistence" in favor of a "detente" or "interdependence" between the U.S. and the Soviet Union, that we should have only parity of military force with the USSR, that the president should trick the American people into unilateral disarmament by a tax cut which would force a decrease in spending on national defense, and that we should seriously consider "unification" of the U.S. and the USSR.

The American people would never vote for State Department Publication 7277, the Rostow Report or the Phoenix Report if given a chance at the polls!

The big question is, can the Johnson administration with help of the New York kingmakers put these policies into effect without the American people realizing it until it is too late?

IV. *The Panama Canal.* In early January 1964, communist-led mobs rioted in Panama and marched on our Panama Canal. The role of Red agents trained by Castro has been confirmed by our secretaries of state and the army.[9] Since Castro's unsuccessful invasion of Panama in 1959, he has built up a cadre of 700 hardcore agents operating inside Panama.[10] After the rioting Khrushchev bellowed:

> Get out before it is too late, before you are chucked out . . . We side with the people of Panama.[11]

The communist apparatus throughout the world echoed the Red line.

What did the Johnson administration do? Did LBJ announce that America's vital interests in the Panama Canal would be defended? Did he tell the world that the Panama Canal is a lawfully-purchased American territory, just like the Louisiana Purchase and Alaska, and that we have been more than generous with the Panamanians?

No, LBJ said on January 23 that the U.S. is willing to engage in "reconsideration of all issues" between the U.S. and Panama and on March 21 to consider "every problem which the Panamanian government wishes to raise."

Americans should beware of the Johnson-Rusk State Department entering into negotiations about the Panama Canal. Based on past history, it looks as though the State Department is softening public opinion for another giveaway of free-world rights and territory that will rank with the tragic Roosevelt and Truman concessions at Teheran, Yalta and Potsdam.

V. *Communist agents in the State Department and the CIA.* State Department Security Officer Scott McLeod listed 648 State Department employees as having had communist activities and associations and ninety-four as perverts. His successor Otto F. Otepka was fired by Dean Rusk for cooperating with the Senate Internal Security Subcommittee. Top Soviet secret police defectors Yuri Nossenko and Michael Goleniewski have described the Red penetration of our State Department and CIA.[12] Congressman Michael Feighan quotes Goleniewski as saying that, when he went to be debriefed by high CIA officials, he found "one of my own agents sitting in front of me."[13] President Johnson and Dean Rusk are trying to sweep these facts under the rug for fear of another Alger Hiss scandal in an election year.

VI. *American jets shot down by the Soviets.* On January 28, 1964 the Russians shot down an unarmed American trainer plane that had wandered over East Germany during a storm. The crew of three was killed. After issuing a perfunctory protest, the next day the State Department announced "the incident is closed."

On March 10 the communists shot down another American plane. Western radar watchers report there have been ninety-five Red violations of Western air space in the last two years. Yet no Red plane has ever been shot down, or even shot at, by the West.

How long will the communists continue to kill Americans and humiliate us before the world? The Johnson Administration has no answer.

VII. *The Oppenheimer Award.* One of Johnson's first acts after becoming President was personally to present the Enrico Fermi Award, which carries with it a tax free purse of $50,000, to J. Robert Oppenheimer.

When anyone tries to say there is no difference between Republicans and Democrats, remember this case of J. Robert Oppenheimer. The Eisenhower administration, with Lewis Strauss as Chairman of the Atomic Energy Commission, revoked Oppenheimer's security clearance. Some of the evidence against Oppenheimer was summarized by William L.

Borden, Executive Director of the Congressional Joint Committee on Atomic Energy, who testified that J. Robert Oppenheimer

> was contributing substantial monthly sums to the Communist Party; . . . his wife and younger brother were Communists; . . . he had at least one Communist mistress . . . he was responsible for employing a number of Communists . . . at wartime Los Alamos . . .[14]

Oppenheimer admitted that he deliberately told a "tissue of lies" to a security officer of the U.S. Army about a contact with him attempted by a Soviet agent.

This is the man whom President Johnson personally presented with the Fermi award and $50,000. Not a single Republican attended the presentation ceremony at the White House.

VIII. *The Edmund Wilson Award*. On December 6, 1963 President Johnson presented the Presidential Medal of Freedom to Edmund Wilson. This is the highest award that any civilian can receive in peacetime. Edmund Wilson's name is unknown to most Americans, so it is appropriate to tell who he is.

He has had four wives.

He is the author of a book so immoral that, even under our contemporary standards, its sale had to be stopped in many places. The banning of his book in New York State was even upheld by the United States Supreme Court.[15]

By his own admission, Edmund Wilson voted the communist ticket in 1932, and the socialist ticket in every other election when Norman Thomas was a candidate.

Edmund Wilson revealed his lack of patriotism in these words from his latest book:

> I have finally come to feel that this coun-
> try, whether or not I continue to live in it,
> is no longer any place for me.[16]

Finally, he did not file any income tax return for nine years. He wrote a book bragging about it called *The Cold War and the Income Tax*.

Yet, one of LBJ's first acts as President was to present a Medal of Freedom to Edmund Wilson.

Failing to file any income tax return is a favorite failing of Democrat liberals. One of the most prominent Democrats of our time, Alben Barkley, failed to file any income tax return for years, including all the time he was Vice President and some of the years he was Majority Leader of the Senate, steering Democrat tax increases through Congress.

Another prominent Democrat liberal who failed to file any income tax return for five years, although his income was more than $60,000 each year, was Dean James Landis, business associate and close personal friend of Joseph P. Kennedy. When the government finally caught up with him, do you think he received the sentence that any ordinary citizen would receive? Certainly not. He was given a thirty-day rest in the finest suite at the most luxurious hospital in New York.[17] Dean Landis held many high government positions under both the New Deal and the New Frontier. Under the Kennedy administration, which was part of the time he failed to file any income tax returns, he was chairman of a special commission to draw up a code of ethics for Government employees.

IX. *The Bobby Baker Case*. President Lyndon Johnson admitted that he accepted from his friend and protégé, Bobby Baker, a hi-fi set that cost $585 wholesale and was worth $800–900 retail. Several years ago Sherman Adams was forced to resign when it was discovered that he had accepted a vicuna coat from Bernard Goldfine. Should not the same principle be applied to LBJ?

Bobby Baker, by his own sworn statement, rose from a net worth of $11,000 to $2,100,000—while he held a full time government job obtained for him by Lyndon Johnson. He received a $100,000 loan from a bank which did not even inquire what his income was. He received a $54,000 loan from the Small Business Administration in circumstances under which no one else would have received a loan.

When called to testify before a Senate Committee, Bobby Baker took the Fifth Amendment many times, as did his secretary whom he falsely listed as his "cousin" in order to evade a District of Columbia zoning regulation.

The public reacted vigorously in the election of 1952 against the mink coats and the deep freezes of the Truman administration. These were minor compared to the insider deals and the extremely valuable favors given to the LBJ radio and television stations by Democratic officeholders.

A popular story of a generation ago concerned an escapee from a nuthouse who, upon learning that the farmers had been ordered by the New Deal to plow under every third row of cotton and to destroy surplus wheat and oranges, exclaimed "Who's looney now?"

There are a number of people in Washington today to whom this expression could apply. Here are a few of the many inconsistencies and contradictions in the policies of the present administration.

While LBJ is turning out the lights in the White House to save a few dollars—he is also turning out the lights of freedom all over the world by spending $44 million on wheat for the communist slavemasters. Who's looney now?

The Johnson administration is sending American boys 9,000 miles away to fight and die against the communists in Vietnam—but the Johnson administration won't do anything at all about the communists only 90 miles away in Cuba. Who's looney now?

The Johnson administration is spending six billion dollars per year to put a man on the moon—and incidentally the space center in Texas is the chief beneficiary of this boondoggle—but the Johnson administration won't send a man to Guantanamo to turn on the water. Who's looney now?

The Democrat administration had a pretended economy drive and closed our forty-five missile bases in Turkey and Italy, cancelled the Skybolt missile, the RS-70 reconnaissance strike bomber, and the Nike-Zeus anti-missile–missile because they are too expensive—but they tell us we can't cut a nickel out of foreign aid to the pro-communist dictators such as Tito and Nkrumah. Who's looney now?

The Democrat administration refused to see the anti-communist Madame Nhu and, while she was visiting in America, gave the green light to her enemies to go ahead and murder her husband[18]—but on the other hand, the Democrat administration lavished millions of dollars of American aid and every possible hospitality on the pro-communist dictator Sukarno, providing him with three call girls (a Latin type, an American type, and a Nordic type) as his travelling companions in violation of the Mann Act.[19] Who's looney now?

When the communists rioted at the Panama Canal, and when the Soviets shot down an American plane killing the crew, LBJ did nothing—but President Johnson went into emergency action and kept Congress in session on Christmas Eve in order to get approval to sell 64 million bushels of wheat to the communists at a price cheaper than Americans pay. Who's looney now?

Many Democrats such as Senators Lausche, Dodd and Thurmond and their millions of supporters do not want to bury the issues of using U.S. tax collections to crush anti-communists in Katanga and Vietnam, and to subsidize the sale and transportation of wheat to our enemies. On March 14, 1964, Senator Lausche told Dean Rusk that such trade "is tantamount to telling the world we've gone to bed with the Communists." And Senator Dodd rejected the attempted distinction Rusk and Under Secretary of State Ball made between Yugoslavia and Poland and other communist nations, saying:

"All of us recognize they're on that side and not on our side."

Because of our two-party system, these anti-communist Democrats are subject to direct and indirect restrictions in their freedom to criticize the Johnson administration. But these anti-communist Democrats hope and pray Republicans will fulfill the chief responsibility of the opposition party—which is to oppose the present administration.

3

Republicans Can't Lose— Unless

With all these issues—issues which are vital to the survival and security of America—issues for which Republicans have the facts and arguments on their side—it looks as though there is no way Republicans can possibly lose *so long as we have a presidential candidate who campaigns on the issues.*

But, the reader may ask, isn't that what a presidential nominee is supposed to do—campaign on the issues? Yes, but let us look at the record and see what actually happened in past campaigns.

In 1940 the Republican candidate, Wendell Willkie, did not campaign on the chief issue of that year, which was Roosevelt's policy of consenting to Stalin's invasions of Poland, Finland, Latvia, Lithuania and Estonia while committing American boys to fight Hitler. When Willkie finally made a few statements on this subject late in the campaign, voters instinctively knew his peace pledges were just "campaign oratory." The second major issue, Roosevelt's violation of the tradition against a third term, was given only superficial mention by Willkie.[1]

In 1944, candidate Thomas Dewey never mentioned the best issue Republicans had that year— how the Roosevelt administration manipulated and invited the disaster at Pearl Harbor by the policy described by Roosevelt's secretary of war as "how we should maneuver the Japs into the position of firing the first shot without allowing too much danger to ourselves." At the personal request of General George Marshall (who was criticized by the Army Pearl Harbor Board for failing to warn the Pearl Harbor command after receiving the decoded Jap war messages), Dewey reneged on Republican plans to make the Pearl Harbor disaster a campaign issue. Dewey lost that year and a whole generation of Americans has grown up ignorant of how World War II began.

In 1948, Republican candidates Thomas Dewey and Earl Warren did not campaign on the major issue of that year, which was communist infiltration in government. The exposure of Alger Hiss, Harry Dexter White and other communists in high government positions had given Republicans their best issue—but Dewey and Warren did not discuss it. By his "Little Sir Echo" campaign, Dewey snatched defeat from the jaws of victory.

In 1952 Republicans were fortunate to have a candidate, Dwight Eisenhower, who squarely faced the issues of that year and approved a hard-hitting campaign. "Corruption, Communism and Korea" were the three dramatic, obvious, winning issues that elected Eisenhower with 55 percent of the popular vote and won a Republican majority in Congress.

In 1956 Republicans again offered the voters a clearcut choice over the liberalism of Adlai Stevenson.

In 1960, Republican candidate Richard Nixon pulled his punches, thereby bringing about another defeat. He never mentioned what informed Republicans considered his best issue: the Senate record of Kennedy and Johnson, including Kennedy's sponsorship of legislation helpful to the communists, namely, the repeal of the loyalty oath provision in the National Defense Education Act, and the repeal of the Battle Act provision which prohibited the sending of strategic materials to Iron Curtain countries, and Johnson's killing of anti-communist legislation such as the bill to restore to the states the right to punish subversion. In the first Nixon-Kennedy television debate (which had the largest audience of all) Kennedy said his objective was "to pick up where FDR left off." Nixon could have told voters where FDR actually left off—at Yalta. But he yielded his right to reply, and lost ground from then until November.

How did it happen that, in four major presidential campaigns, Republicans were maneuvered into nominating candidates who did not campaign on the major issues?

It wasn't any accident. It was planned that way. In each of their losing presidential years, a small group of secret kingmakers, using hidden persuaders and psychological warfare techniques, manipulated the Republican National Convention to nominate candidates who would sidestep or suppress the key issues.

The kingmakers and their propaganda apparatus have launched a series of false slogans designed to mask the failure of their candidates to debate the major issues. Some of these are the following: "Politics should stop at the water's edge." "We must unite behind our president who has sole power in the field of foreign affairs." "Foreign policy should be bipartisan." In the words of one great Republican leader, "Bipartisanship is just a $5 word for . . . a two-bit word, 'me-tooism.'"[2]

The real motive behind these false and dangerous slogans is that the secret kingmakers do not want the New Deal-New Frontier foreign policy—in which they have a vested interest—debated, investigated, or submitted to the voters. Republicans should recognize the truth of the testament handed down by Senator Robert A. Taft shortly before his death:

> We cannot clean up the mess in Washington, balance the budget, reduce taxes, check creeping Socialism, tell what is muscle or fat in our sprawling rearmament programs, purge subversives from our State Department, unless we come to grips with our foreign policy, upon which all other policies depend.

Politics makes strange bedfellows. The secret kingmakers have made common cause with the Democrats who had everything to gain and nothing to lose if the Republicans made a weak campaign.

One of the favorite tricks of the Democrats is to try to get the Republicans to pass over their strongest candidate and nominate instead a candidate who will be easy to beat. For example, in 1948 the Democrats cooperated with the kingmakers to persuade Republicans to nominate a "me too" losing candidate, Tom Dewey, instead of the Republican Majority Leader, Bob Taft. The Democrats said they "hoped Republicans would nominate Taft" with the same reverse psychology that Brer Rabbit pleaded with the fox, "Oh, please don't throw me into the briar patch!"

After the 1948 election, the Democrats bragged about the trick they had pulled. Jack Redding, former publicity director of the Democratic National Committee, in his book *Inside the Democratic Party*, quoted Democratic National Chairman Robert Hannegan as saying in a Democratic strategy huddle:

> If the Republicans were smart, they'd run Taft. He'd make a better candidate and would probably be harder for us to beat because he would fight harder. Don't make the mistake of underestimating Taft. The fact is Taft is a fighter and will make a terrific fight for what he represents. Dewey will be 'me too' all over again . . . Hit Taft hard and often; maybe we can stop him from getting the nomination and at the same time embarrass Dewey.

Harold Ickes put it more bluntly. He said:

> With the bases loaded, the Republicans sent to the plate their bat boy. They could have sent in their Babe Ruth—Bob Taft.

The question for Republicans at their 1964 National Convention was: At this crucial point in American history, will we send in our bat boy? Or will we send in our Babe Ruth—a man who is not afraid or forbidden to take a good cut at all major issues of the day?

America is best served when the two great political parties compete with one another to the fullest possible extent consistent with ethical conduct. It was in the forum of vigorous political debate that the United States Constitution was hammered out by the Founding Fathers. Abraham Lincoln rose to greatness from the platform of hard-hitting partisan debates with Stephen A. Douglas over issues that were just as important to our country's survival as any issues today.

The secret of Anglo-American justice is the competitive, adversarial trial system. Truth is best served and favoritism eliminated by a procedure which requires the litigants to compete to their maximum ability. There would be no justice in our courts if opposing lawyers went through an Alphonse and Gaston "me too" performance and agreed with their opponents on key points.

Free competition has been the secret of America's greatness. Honest competition between our producers, our transporters, our merchants, has made the American economic system the envy of the world.

With only one-fifteenth of the world's population, we produce over one-half of the world's goods. As sponsor of the great Sherman Anti-Trust Law, the Republican Party is especially dedicated to preserving and fostering competition.

Like trials, political campaigns should be competitive and adversarial. The Republican Party has a historic duty to demand that the major parties compete on foreign policy issues. Failure to compete in this field means a coverup of past mistakes. Free debate in this field will help us to avoid the same mistakes in the future and enable American voters to make the right choice on the basis of all the facts.

4

The Smoke-Filled Room

1936

I n early 1936 a little group of secret kingmakers laid long-range plans to control the Republican Party. Their confidential meeting was in keeping with the political legend of the smoke-filled hotel room.

The presiding genius of this secret gathering in a royal suite on the tweny-first floor of the Waldorf-Astoria Hotel in New York was Thomas Lamont, senior partner in J. P. Morgan and Company, well-known international banking concern. Lamont was flanked to the right and left by Thomas Cochran, also of the Morgan firm, and by Alfred P. Sloan of General Motors. Five other prominent financiers and industrialists were also present.

The purpose of this august gathering was to consider possible Republican candidates for president against Franklin D. Roosevelt, who was then near-ing the end of his first term.

We know from an account of this meeting by Dr. Glenn Frank,[1] president of the University of Wisconsin, who was present that the men in this select group spoke with the assurance that they would "decide" who the Republican nominee for president would be. The midwest was clamoring for recognition, and the eastern elite had decided that they would support a candidate from the corn belt.

Before the night was out, it was pretty well agreed that their support would be thrown to Governor Alf Landon of Kansas, who, of course, never stood a chance to win, because there was no beating Roosevelt for reelection in 1936.

One of the kingmakers at this secret meeting summed up the purpose of the meeting in these words:

> In the event we are not successful this year, we will select the candidate for 1940, and he will come from the East.

Support for Landon by the Lamont clique was sop for the midwest in a hopeless Republican year. The real goal was 1940 when, with the midwest presumably satisfied, the East would claim the right to name the nominee.

The choice of Landon was a significant one. The kingmakers such as "Ogden Mills, Eugene Meyer, Winthrop Aldrich recognized that . . . Landon might be adapted to their own purposes."[2] Landon had boasted, "I have cooperated with the New Deal to the best of my ability," and had even issued public praise of New Deal radical Rexford G. Tugwell.[3] It was not mere coincidence that the kingmakers passed over Herbert Hoover as too conservative, and vetoed Colonel Frank Knox for first place on the ticket because, although a liberal, he had attacked Marxism and Socialism in the New Deal.

When Landon was buried under an avalanche of electoral votes in 1936, the New York kingmakers breathed a collective sigh of relief that the Republican Party had escaped passing into control of the midwest.

5

The Advertising Agent's Holiday

1940

As the 1940 election approached, the secret kingmakers met again in a hotel room in the Waldorf-Astoria in New York to decide who would be the Republican presidential candidate that year. They wanted someone who would be their willing tool, and whom they could rely on not to change or challenge the Roosevelt foreign policy. If their eastern candidate could have the "image" of a midwesterner, this would help to sell him to Republicans.

Suddenly someone suggested a New York lawyer named Wendell Willkie.

The kingmakers paused to think about the possibility of Wendell Willkie. He was a registered Democrat. Only five years before, he had been elected by Tammany Hall to the New York County Democratic

Committee![1] As a student at Indiana University, he had been a member of the Socialist Club.[2] He had never done anything in his entire life for the Republican Party. He was completely unknown outside his own limited circles. He was the high-salaried head of a large utility company. He had risen in the world as a lawyer who had successfully defended a large public utilities corporation against hundreds of personal-injury damage suits.

With all these handicaps, it was unthinkable that such a man, with such a background, could receive the highest honor the Republican Party confers. Unthinkable, that is, unless you know the power of the secret kingmakers and the "hidden persuaders" they are able to wield through their financial and propaganda contacts.

In spite of all his liabilities, the kingmakers decided Willkie was their man. They went to work to sell Willkie to the American public by a gigantic publicity spree. The columnist George Sokolsky called it "the advertising agent's holiday." Through their financial and other contacts throughout our communications media, they made it appear there was spontaneous public interest in Wendell Willkie.

Willkie was catapulted into the political arena by an article in the *Saturday Evening Post*. The big buildup gained momentum as articles suggesting Willkie for the Republican nomination suddenly began to appear in leading newspapers and magazines. His picture spontaneously appeared on the covers of *Time* and other popular magazines. He was given prestige in business circles by a favorable article in *Fortune*, and in popular circles by a feature article in *Life*. This unknown lawyer mysteriously appeared as an author in Sunday magazines.

There was no television in 1940, but there was radio, and the most popular program was "Information Please," then at the peak of its Hooper rating and boasting 12 million listeners. It was arranged for Wendell Willkie to be a guest on "Information Please," where he surprised everyone by having his hand up more often and answering more questions than all the experts, even John Kieran. This radio program was loaded with technical questions about the United States Constitution, which were tailored for Willkie, the only lawyer on the panel.

On the chance that this program might be successful, the kingmakers were farsighted enough to have many pictures and a movie short made of it. After editing, the movie was shown in neighborhood movies all over the United States, and *Life* magazine of April 22 featured a full page of pictures showing Willkie outsmarting all the intellectuals.

The Willkie boom was engineered by top advertising executives from Madison Avenue public relations firms such as Young and Rubicam, J. Walter

Thompson, and Selvage and Smith.[3] Working individually and collectively, these publicity men planted news articles in magazines and newspapers, stimulated petitions, chain letters, advertisements, telegrams and fund-raising, and started Willkie Clubs and Willkie Mailing Committees. The advertising manager of Johns-Manville organized the Indiana Box Supper to promote the legend of Willkie's rural background.

Seven weeks before the Republican Convention, the Gallup Poll reported that Willkie was the favorite of only three per cent of Republican voters. Like the new cold remedies on the market each winter, advertising turned Willkie into a 60-day wonder.

In 1940 the two leading contenders for the Republican nomination were Thomas E. Dewey and Senator Robert A. Taft. The New York kingmakers considered Dewey an unacceptable candidate because, in those days, Dewey was an isolationist who stressed his Michigan birth and education.

Governor Harold Stassen of Minnesota had declared himself for Dewey and had invited Dewey into the Minnesota primary and even helped Dewey finance his campaign there. The kingmakers looked upon the Minnesota situation as a significant obstacle to Willkie because a defeat there could be dangerous to Willkie's midwestern image.

The kingmakers are very resourceful, and it didn't take them long to solve this problem. Thomas Lamont discovered he had a relative named John Cowles, who was publisher of the *Minneapolis Star*, a large newspaper strategically important to Stassen's future. After a few telephone calls, it was suggested to Stassen that he go to New York and confer with some very important people.

A delectable plum was dangled in front of the ambitious Stassen: he was told he had been selected to be Temporary Chairman of the Republican National Convention, in which capacity he would deliver the Keynote Speech. In a few days Stassen returned to Minnesota—no longer supporting Tom Dewey.

In order to receive the appointment as Temporary Chairman and Keynoter of the Convention, Stassen had to give a pledge to the Republican National Committee that he would remain neutral between all candidates for the nomination. Somehow this promise was forgotten; Stassen was so unneutral that he even served as Willkie's Floor Manager during the convention. This was the first of many chores that Stassen has performed for the secret kingmakers.

As Convention time approached, one big stumbling block remained for Wendell Willkie—Senator Robert A. Taft. Knowledgeable observers could see that the race had narrowed itself to Willkie and Taft. Thinking that perhaps they might not be able to put Willkie over after all, and always wanting to have an alternate candidate waiting in the wings, the kingmakers decided to make a try at buying Taft.

The week before the Convention opened, Senator and Mrs. Taft were invited to a dinner party in New York given by Mr. and Mrs. Ogden Reid, publisher of the *New York Herald Tribune*. The details of the dinner party are set forth in *One Man: Wendell Willkie* by C. Nelson Sparks. The major facts have been thoroughly corroborated by both Robert Taft and Wendell Willkie.

The guest list for the Ogden Reid dinner party was carefully chosen. Present at this momentous dinner party were Mr. Thomas Lamont, senior partner of J. P. Morgan Company, and Mrs. Lamont; Lord Lothian, then Ambassador to the United States from Great Britain; Mr. and Mrs. John Pillsbury of the Minneapolis milling family; and Mr. and Mrs. Wendell Willkie. It was an elegant dinner party, featuring the choicest duck served in the highest style, with a liveried lackey to wait on each guest.

Over cigars and coffee, the small talk was suddenly interrupted when the hostess announced that those present would be favored with a few remarks from Lord Lothian. The substance of his little speech was that it was the duty of the United

States to go all out at once to aid Britain in the war. This was in June of 1940, a year and a half before Pearl Harbor. Thomas Lamont was then called on, and he expressed himself as fully in accord with Lord Lothian. Willkie was called on next. He enthusiastically endorsed everything that Lord Lothian and Lamont had said. Willkie went all out for war, maintaining that it was our duty to go to war at once to aid England.

By this time, the plot was pretty clear to Taft. He realized that he had been invited to the Reid dinner for the purpose of ascertaining whether he were willing to pay the price to get the support of the secret kingmakers for the Republican nomination, namely, an all-out war declaration that would satisfy the New York banking interests and the British Ambassador. Taft knew that if he endorsed the remarks of Lothian, Lamont and Willkie, he would make himself acceptable to the powerful financial interests and thereby greatly improve his chance of winning the nomination.

Taft was a man of principle and he declined this rare opportunity to win the support of the kingmakers. When called on, he simply observed that he could add nothing to his remarks in the Senate, where he declared that Americans did not want to go to war to beat a totalitarian system in Europe if they were to get socialism here when it is all over.

Then Senator and Mrs. Taft left the party as soon as they could gracefully do so. A few days later, the *New York Herald Tribune* announced its unequivocal support for Wendell Willkie with a three-column appeal to the delegates on the front page calling Willkie "Heaven's gift to the nation in its time of crisis."

When the Republican National Convention opened in Philadelphia, Willkie only had 105 delegates. Even the Gallup Poll reported that Willkie was the favorite of only 17% of Republicans. Only the politically naive could believe that hundreds of delegates suddenly went overboard for Willkie out of sheer fascination with the gravel voice and personality of "the barefoot boy from Wall Street."

A few Republicans saw through the publicity blitz at the time. Forty Republican congressmen called for a "real Republican." Congressman Usher Burdick declared:

> I believe I am serving the best interests
> of the Republican Party by protesting in
> advance and exposing the machinations
> and attempts of J. P. Morgan and the
> other New York utility bankers in forcing
> Wendell Willkie on the Republican Party
> . . . There is nothing to the Willkie boom
> for President except the artificial public
> opinion being created by newspapers,

magazines, and the radio. The reason back of all this is money. Money is being spent by someone and lots of it. This is a good time to find out whether the American people are to be let alone in the selection of a Republican candidate for the Presidency, or whether the 'special interests' of this country are powerful enough to dictate to the American people.[4]

Willkie had the support of the New York kingmakers whose long fingers of money and propaganda reached into every state. Their propaganda buildup for Willkie began to pay off in Philadelphia where Thomas Lamont set up headquarters. In addition, the kingmakers opened their bag of tricks for use at the convention itself. The "hidden persuaders" really went into action.

The "get on the bandwagon" psychology was played to the nth degree. The galleries were packed with noisy Willkie supporters admitted on forged tickets who chanted "we want Willkie" to stampede the convention. This chant was used with the same repetition technique that advertisers developed for cigarettes.

Five-dollar bills were given to taxi drivers to talk up Willkie. When delegates would grab a cab to the convention hall and ask the driver the obvious question, "How do things look?" the driver would reply, "It looks like everything is going to Willkie."

"Operation Telegram" was the most successful gimmick of the Willkie blitz. Nearly a million wires poured into Philadelphia for Willkie between Saturday and Tuesday.[5] In many of the larger cities all over the United States a few days before the convention opened, pleasant female voices were calling prominent citizens and saying, "This is Western Union calling. Would you let us send the following telegram to your delegates at the convention in Philadelphia in behalf of Wendell Willkie?" The people called were prominent or important financially, but not politically wise. They were flattered at the thought of mixing in a small way with stirring political events. They did not realize they were paying for the telegrams; but they found them later on their phone bills.

Another phase of "Operation Telegram" was to shower a delegate with wires from his clients or customers back home. For example, one delegate was a successful automobile dealer who had gone to the convention pledged to vote for another candidate. He received a telegram advocating Willkie's nomination from almost every man or woman to whom he had sold a Packard automobile. Many telegrams were not sent by the persons whose names were signed to them, and wires from all over the country showed unusual similarity in wording and misspellings. After the delegate returned home and inquired, it was too late.

The kingmakers sought to influence delegates by having the mortgage holders and bankers to whom they owed money call them in behalf of Willkie.[6] For example, one delegate was called long distance by a miller in his home town who had annually advanced him money and seed on his season's crops. The miller, a Democrat, demanded that the delegate vote for Willkie. Later the same day, the delegate's banker who held the mortgage on his farm, called with the same demand. The delegate voted for Willkie because he felt he had to.

The Willkie campaign was richly-financed, and money was spent freely before and during the convention. The chairman of one delegation stated that he was offered $19,000 for the expenses of his delegation if he would deliver his state's vote for Willkie.[7] Another state was told to name its own price as payment for announcing a switch to Willkie. Powerful economic interests brought pressures on state delegations to force officeholders in line if they wanted to keep their jobs.

And so, the blitz was a success. The Republican Party, in convention assembled, nominated Wendell Willkie for the presidency, with Taft a close second and Dewey farther behind. Willkie had no grassroots appeal and he ran a poor race, trailing the rest of the Republican ticket in most states. He failed to carry eleven states which at the same time elected Republican governors. His showing was pitiful in spite of the fact that he had the support of a long procession of prominent Democrats including two former Democratic presidential nominees, John W. Davis and Alfred E. Smith; former FDR braintrusters General Hugh Johnson and Raymond Moley; and many Democratic governors and senators. In no election since the Civil War had so many party leaders deserted their own party for the opposition. Many other senior Democrats were hostile to Roosevelt, but silent to preserve their party membership, including James A. Farley and Vice President John Garner.

After the election, Willkie was exposed as a complete phony. He cynically admitted under oath to a Senate committee that pledges he had made before the election were just "campaign oratory."[8] He hired an identified Soviet agent to ghost-write his book *One World*. He eagerly donated his legal services to defend a top communist named Schneiderman and take his case to the United States Supreme Court.

Those who might think Willkie's defeat bothered the New York kingmakers who had blitzed his nomination, just don't understand politics. The kingmakers did not care whether Willkie won or lost. All they cared was to make sure that they had on both tickets an eastern interventionist candidate who would continue Roosevelt's foreign policy so that the voters would not have a choice on the great issue of entering the European War. Their objective was to make sure that, if by chance a Republican should win, he would be a man the secret kingmakers could control. Their attitude was like that of the old time Philadelphia political boss who, when told his candidate could not win and would wreck the party, replied: "Yes, but we will own the wreckage."

6

The Pollsters and the Hoaxers

1944

The New York kingmakers realized they could not capture the 1944 Republican nomination either with Willkie or with the same type of last-minute blitz they had used in 1940. This time they went into action earlier. They discovered and developed a new political weapon: the Gallup Poll. Dr. George Gallup began asking a lot of questions of a very few people, and—funny thing—he usually came up with answers that pleased the New York kingmakers.

The Gallup Poll has been used repeatedly as a subtle propaganda machine to sell the Republicans on the false propositions that the GOP cannot win unless it (1) continues the New Deal foreign policy and (2) names candidates who will appeal to left-leaning Democrats and liberals.

The Gallup Poll worked so well that, in 1944, there was hardly any need to have a Republican Convention. The Gallup Poll had already announced that Dewey had 68 percent of Republican voters in his camp, and that he was the only Republican with a chance to win. The convention was cold, dull and colorless. The delegates met merely to ratify the Gallup Poll decision.

Why did the kingmakers support Dewey in 1944 when they had fought him in 1940? Very simple. Dewey observed what happened in 1940 and how one gets to be the Republican nominee. Dewey decided to pay the price that Senator Taft had refused to pay at the Ogden Reid dinner. Dewey abandoned his isolationist views, joined with the New York internationalists, and became one of the powerful kingmakers himself.

It may be that, with World War II in full swing, no Republican could have been elected that year. Nevertheless, Dewey made a weak campaign and refused to mention, because of the personal request of George Marshall,[1] the best issue the Republicans had: how Roosevelt had invited and encouraged the Pearl Harbor attack. Dewey knew that Roosevelt had refused to negotiate with the pro-American government of Prince Konoye of Japan, and had given its successor an ultimatum which meant war. Dewey knew that we had broken the top Japanese code before Pearl Harbor. He knew that President Roosevelt, his secretaries of war and navy, and his Chief of Staff George Marshall, had advance warnings of the Japanese attack. He knew that Pearl Harbor was a disaster for which the commander-in-chief should be held personally responsible. Yet, he said nothing—and the voters failed to learn the truth.

After the votes were counted, the Roosevelt foreign policy was safe again from any effective challenge for four years. Roosevelt traveled to Yalta where he sold out our allies in Eastern Europe and China, and gave Stalin three votes in the United Nations.

7

Snatching Defeat from the Jaws of Victory

1948

The 1948 Republican nomination was a coveted prize. Two years earlier, the slogan "Had Enough?" and public reaction to price controls had given the Republican Party its largest victory of our time. On the principle that "coming events cast their shadows before them," Republicans confidently anticipated a sure win.

There was much resentment among conservative Republicans against the "me too" campaign Dewey had waged in 1944. There was a strong Republican Party tradition against nominating a loser, on the principle best expressed by Theodore Roosevelt's daughter, Alice Longworth, that "you can't make a souffle rise twice." But the Gallup Poll again hoaxed Republicans into nominating the choice of the New York kingmakers, Thomas E. Dewey.

To secure the nomination, the Dewey forces spent money and made deals and promises that Taft would never make. Offers were made of federal jobs that delegates could not resist. Mississippi's delegation was headed by a Taft man, but his delegates voted the other way. After the vote, one delegate ran for a train and died of a heart attack on it. He had $1,500 in fresh money on him and the other delegates claimed it should be divided among them.[1]

One of the deals made by the Dewey managers was with Congressman Charles Halleck, who was promised the vice presidential nomination if he could deliver the Indiana delegation to Dewey. It wasn't easy, but Halleck delivered, confident that he would have second place on the ticket.

In the hours after Dewey was nominated President, the New York kingmakers, determined to continue the Roosevelt foreign policy, stepped in to scotch the deal. Speaking through their house organ, the *New York Times*, the kingmakers declared:

> Surely not Mr. Halleck! Mr. Halleck would bring into the campaign the perfect record of a Republican isolationist. Mr. Halleck voted against Selective Service in the summer of 1940 . . . Mr. Halleck voted against Lend-Lease . . . He

> voted against the British loan. He voted
> against the Hull reciprocal trade pro-
> gram in 1940 . . . With Mr. Taber he led
> the fight to cut appropriations under the
> Marshall Plan . . .

Here was a good summary of what kind of a candidate the New York kingmakers will not tolerate.
They will not permit a candidate on the ticket—
even in second place—unless he has a foreign policy
acceptable to the New York financiers and banking
interests who profit so greatly from the New Deal
foreign policy.

Dewey and the kingmakers chose Earl Warren of
California as the vice presidential nominee. Before
starting out on the campaign trail, Dewey and Warren promised each other that neither would mention the hottest issue of the day—the one on which
the Democrats were most vulnerable—the issue of
communist infiltration in the federal government.

Even with the benefit of 20/20 hindsight, it is
hard to see how Dewey could have lost. The Democrats were hopelessly split, with the Southerners
supporting Strom Thurmond and the left-wing radi-
cals supporting Henry Wallace.

Truman pitched his campaign against the Republican 80th Congress. Dewey made a fatal mistake
when he did not defend it. The Republican 80th

Congress, under the leadership of Senator Robert Taft, had made the greatest record of any Congress in the 20th century. For the first time since the start of the New Deal, it reduced taxes, balanced the budget, and reduced the national debt. It exposed Alger Hiss, Harry Dexter White and other communists in the New Deal. It launched the Greek-Turkish Military Aid Plan which under General Van Fleet crushed the communist guerillas in Greece. It enacted the Taft-Hartley Law over Truman's veto. It rejected Truman's plan to draft railroad strikers into the Army. It authorized the Hoover Commission to reorganize the government. It passed the Twenty-second Amendment to the Constitution limiting the president to two terms. By any standard, it was a constructive, responsible Congress, and would have been a winning issue for Republicans.

By his incredible "me too" campaign, by his refusal to debate the issues of the 80th Congress and communism in government, Dewey truly snatched defeat from the jaws of victory.[2] Republicans found to their sorrow that Dewey could not Gallup into the White House as he had Galluped into the nomination.

But again, Dewey's defeat did not bother the kingmakers at all. All they wanted was to make sure there was a candidate on both tickets who would rubberstamp their America Last foreign policy.

The 1948 election results should have destroyed the Gallup Poll as a weapon which could again capture the presidential nomination. Gallup predicted that Dewey would be elected in a landslide. Leading liberal opinion-makers such as Walter Lippmann were so carried away by misplaced confidence in Gallup that they suggested we dispense with the election, save that national expense, and simply declare Dewey the winner over Truman.

It is time the American people wake up to the inaccuracy of the Gallup Poll. In ancient times, superstitious people used to go to the temple and beg a prophecy from some priestess who belonged to an elite cult. The batting average of these ancient frauds was at least as good as the Gallup Poll. The famous Delphic Oracle built up a phony reputation as a prophet by giving trick answers subject to contradictory interpretations. To the question: Who will win the war between Athens and Sparta, the Oracle answered: "I say to you Sparta, the Athenians will conquer."

Likewise, the Gallup Poll has built its reputation by asking trick questions. Ask a loaded question and get a loaded answer.

Author and political analyst Svend Petersen made a thorough statistical analysis of the presidential polls taken by George Gallup and compared them with the presidential polls taken by the old

Literary Digest which went out of existence after predicting that Landon would defeat Roosevelt in 1936. His conclusion: the *Literary Digest* scored three victories and one failure; the Gallup Poll achieved one victory, one failure, and in two elections Gallup reported such a large percentage of voters "who had not made up their minds" that his poll could not be called either a success or failure.[3]

It is too bad for American politics that the Gallup Poll did not have the good grace (like the *Literary Digest*) after its abysmal failure in 1948, to fold its tent and silently steal away.

It should be noted that the *Literary Digest* polled millions, while George Gallup polls only a few hundred—so few that the exact number is a dark secret which Gallup will not reveal. Were he to reveal the pathetic paucity of his pollees, the myth of the Gallup Poll would join the myth of the Delphic Oracle in the limbo of history.

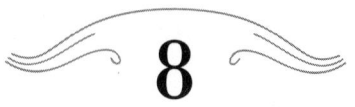

8

The Big Steal

1952

For long in advance, it was easy for everyone to see that 1952 would be a crucial election year, and a good year for Republicans. The Truman scandals, the Korean War, communist infiltration in government, the fact that for the first time since 1932 the GOP was not faced with an incumbent President—all these factors combined to make the Republican nomination an even greater prize than in 1948.

The obvious choice was Senator Robert A. Taft, the man who was the acknowledged leader of the Republican Party in good years as well as bad, who had one of the most honorable and distinguished records of government service of any man alive, who was respected by both friends and enemies, who was the choice of the overwhelming majority of organization Republicans.

The kingmakers vetoed Taft. It has been said that "Hell hath no fury like a woman scorned." What the American public was to learn in 1952 was that "Hell hath no fury like the New York kingmakers scorned." Taft had scorned them at the Ogden Reid dinner party in 1940. The kingmakers knew he was not one of them. They could not control him. He was dedicated to reduce the level of federal spending. Most important, he would never condone the America Last policy of the New Deal. Taft's own book *A Foreign Policy for Americans* was based on this simple premise (which was anathema to the kingmakers):

> The ultimate purpose of our foreign policy must be to protect the liberty of the people of the United States.

The kingmakers' propagandists launched a potent word missile: "I like Taft, but Taft can't win." This slogan was cleverly designed to drive a wedge between Taft and his supporters, and it probably did affect many people. Of course it was completely false, as Taft had the best vote-getting record of any Republican in the country, and had proved this ability in Ohio in his tremendous 1950 victory, in spite of dire predictions to the contrary. During the preferential primaries held in 1952, Taft polled more popular votes than any other Republican candidate.

The kingmakers selected their 1952 candidate carefully—General Dwight Eisenhower. It should be made perfectly clear that nothing in these pages is meant to cast any reflection whatsoever on Eisenhower. He was an amateur in politics; he did not have the slightest idea of the tactics used by the little clique determined to steal the nomination and push him into the presidency.

Eisenhower was a long-time favorite of the kingmakers. Several years before, they had placed him in an important non-political job to keep him in the public eye, but not require him to take a stand on controversial questions such as the Taft-Hartley Act and communists in our government. They had installed him as president of Columbia University. With all due respect to Ike's many talents, he was not suited for this position. Yet, the kingmakers found Ike's lack of qualifications no handicap, because some of the kingmakers were trustees of Columbia University.

In order to make sure they retained control of the 96-vote New York delegation at the 1952 Republican National Convention, the kingmakers persuaded Thomas E. Dewey to run for a third term as governor of New York in 1950. By orders of Winthrop Aldrich of the Chase National (Rockefeller) Bank,

Lieutenant Governor Joe R. Hanley, who was to have been the candidate, was bludgeoned into withdrawing. Hanley revealed in a letter which leaked out that he had been "humiliated" and was "disappointed and heartsick" over the pressure put on him, but he had withdrawn on the promise that his debts would be paid and he would be given a fat state job.

The secret kingmakers never put all their eggs in one basket. They always have a stand-in waiting in the wings. Just on the outside chance that they might not be able to sell Ike to the Republican Party, they had placed their second choice, Harold Stassen, on ice as president of the University of Pennsylvania. Stassen was even less qualified to be a university president than Eisenhower.

The New York kingmakers reactivated the whole propaganda apparatus that they had created to publicize Wendell Willkie. The Madison Avenue public relations firms, the big national magazines, and four-fifths of the influential newspapers in the country turned themselves into propaganda organs to build the Eisenhower image. For months and months, Ike's picture was on the cover of magazines and we were inundated with articles proposing him for the Republican nomination.

But even all this fantastic propaganda buildup, arranged through the diverse financial contacts of the New York kingmakers, could not have won the nomination for Eisenhower had it not been for the vicious and dishonest "hidden persuaders" used just prior to and during the convention itself. Of course thousands of sincere people were genuinely for Eisenhower; just as thousands of sincere people were for General Douglas MacArthur. The point is that Eisenhower could not have been successful without the vicious tactics used by the New York kingmakers determined to destroy Taft.

These tactics started early in 1952 in the New Hampshire primary, although we didn't learn about these "hidden persuaders" until long after. Ike-supporter Tex McCrary himself admitted that he had used dirty tactics against Taft in that crucial primary. He said:

> I planted people in every Taft audience. I would have mothers get up to say, "I have a son who is being drafted—and he wants to ask you why your voting record is the same as Marcantonio's."

Of course this was a loaded question, as Taft's voting record was the opposite of pro-communist Marcantonio. But such tactics had their effect, and New Hampshire was Taft's first setback.[1]

Taft was beset by repeated attacks that had no regard for truth and decency. Arthur Hays

Sulzberger, publisher of the *New York Times*, said that his newspaper was opposing Taft's presidential nomination "because it is so frightened at the thought of Mr. Taft."[2]

As time for the Republican Convention approached, it became apparent that Taft had enough delegates to win the nomination on the first ballot. Eisenhower was at least 150 delegates short. The New York kingmakers were desperate. They had to come up with some trick, some gimmick, some "hidden persuader," to capture a crucial few delegates from Taft.

The opportunity presented itself in Texas. They devised a scheme whereby they would ignore the legally-elected Taft delegates, hold rump meetings to which they would invite Democrats who had no intention of voting for any Republican in the November election, and have this illegal body "elect" Eisenhower delegates, who would then try to unseat the Taft delegates at the convention.

The Eisenhower managers ran advertisements in Texas newspapers, and mailed vast quantities of postcards addressed to "Occupant," which invited Democrats to come to Republican Party meetings and "vote" for Eisenhower. These ads stated: "You are not pledged to support the nominee of the Republican Party nor does it prohibit you from voting in the July Democratic Primary nor does it prohibit you from voting for whomever you please in the November election."

These advertisements fraudulently represented that Democrats—who intended to remain Democrats—could elect delegates to the Republican National Convention. Such a procedure was clearly contrary to Texas law. The advertisements and postcards urged voters to do what Texas law expressly prohibits.

(One of the reasons why this is wrong was aptly stated by one Republican: "If this procedure were allowed, all Republicans would need to do to win would be to send their members into Democratic primaries and party conventions and nominate Alger Hiss!")

When Taft and his supporters protested this illegal action, one of the kingmakers' hatchet men came up with a brainstorm—accuse Taft of stealing delegates!

The first newspaper to shout "the big steal" was the *Houston Post*, whose owner, Oveta Culp Hobby, was later rewarded by appointment as Secretary of Health, Education and Welfare. Suddenly, as though someone had pressed a button, the whole propaganda apparatus of our country went into action to slander the character of the most honorable man in public life. Our whole communications media echoed with the slogan "Thou shalt not steal."

The "big steal" issue was expanded to take in Georgia and Louisiana, too. *Time* magazine came out with a special edition on Monday of convention week so that every delegate could be provided with the issue accusing Taft of the "big steal." Masked bandits with guns paraded the streets of Chicago carrying placards which read "Taft steals votes," and oversize signs appeared proclaiming RAT stands for Robert A. Taft.

How the liberal press picked up and spread the smear against Taft can be best described in the words of Allen Drury in *Advise and Consent*:

> All the vast publicity machine that always goes into concerted action for a liberal cause had gone to work . . . ; an operation so honed and smoothed and refined over the years that none of its proprietors even had to consult with one another. The instinct had been alerted, the bell had rung, the national salivations had come forth on schedule.

Eisenhower had no real knowledge of the tactics used by his supporters to steal the nomination. When he learned of what was happening in Texas, he stated at a press conference: "I myself would never have put in such advertisement in such a paper."[3] This, in effect, constituted a repudiation of all the claims of "dishonesty" and "fraud" made by Henry Cabot Lodge, Sherman Adams and the Eisenhower managers. This, in effect, was an admission by Eisenhower that it was his own supporters who were guilty of fraud in Texas.

When the illegally-elected Eisenhower delegates arrived at the Republican National Convention in Chicago, the job was to get them officially seated in place of the Taft delegates, in order to take away Taft's narrow margin of victory. By high-pressure propaganda and hypocritical bleating about the moral issue, the kingmakers brought about a change in the rules under which every previous convention had functioned. Although this rules change was contrary to common sense as well as every principle of parliamentary procedure, it was called the "fair play amendment."

After the rules were changed, the second battle at the 1952 Convention was over the seating of the contested delegates. By promising Earl Warren the first appointment to the Supreme Court and Richard Nixon the vice presidency, the kingmakers persuaded the California delegation—without hearing any of the evidence—to vote to expel the Georgia, Louisiana and Texas delegates and seat the Eisenhower delegates.

The California delegation, as well as the New York and other crucial delegations, were told to vote for the Eisenhower delegates in the contests, regardless of the merits of the case, regardless of the evidence, regardless of the judicial determinations of party conventions in the states and supporting court decisions, regardless of the hours of open hearings in the Republican Party's own tribunals, the National Committee and the Credentials Committee. This was called "fair play."

The pressure put on delegates on the issue of the contested delegates was apparent to spectators at the hearings held by the Credentials Committee. The Pennsylvania representative on this committee was a fair-minded judge who, although in the Eisenhower camp, voted to award the contested delegates to Taft because he believed that was the just verdict after hearing the evidence. The following day, he returned to the hearing and reversed his vote. Pressure from Governor John S. Fine had turned him into a shaken and humiliated man, required to vote against his conscience. Fine himself had been brought into line by the kingmakers with the promise that he could dispense all federal patronage in Pennsylvania.[4]

Tom Dewey was there reminding his New York delegation that he would remain governor for another two and a half years, and that he had "a long memory."[5] He reminded the delegates of the control he had over state jobs. Any delegate who disobeyed Dewey had to be prepared to lose his job, or have his relative or friend lose his job. Taft had pledges from seventeen New York delegates but, after the Dewey ukase, only four dared to vote for Taft on the contested delegates, the same courageous four who had attended General Douglas MacArthur's Keynote Speech on the first night of the convention, in defiance of Dewey's orders. None of the other ninety-two Dewey-controlled delegates was permitted to attend the Keynote Speech of the convention they were elected to participate in.

Sherman Adams was there, presumably making the same kind of deals with state delegations that he later made with Bernard Goldfine for a vicuna coat and a Turkish rug. Winthrop Aldrich, president of the Chase National Bank, was there; for his pre-convention services he was appointed Ambassador to England. Henry Ford II was there, with his yacht in Lake Michigan equipped to entertain wavering delegates, and to provide a fleet of Mercuries with drivers for the use of pro-Ike delegates. Eisenhower managers whispered that delegates who held out for Taft would be marked for life.

When the convention opened, the Taft headquarters had the signed pledges of 604 delegates, the narrow majority he needed out of 1,203. Eisenhower had only 400 plus. But the attrition of the "hidden persuaders" whittled away at Taft's majority and cost the margin of victory. The Taft headquarters received reports of delegates who were bodily put on the train for home, leaving their alternates to vote for Ike. Delegates were threatened with loss of their jobs and calling of their bank loans, unless they voted for Eisenhower. Money flowed in great quantities everywhere.

One of the Chicago newspapers summed up the convention like this:

> While yelling, "Steal!" they stole. While piously condemning evil, they entered the bagnio with it. With holy airs, they prejudged the issues, and with piety—and a hope of patronage—they cried corruption while corrupting their own small souls. It was a sickening spectacle.
>
> On Monday the cry was "fair play." On Wednesday all pretense of fairness was forsaken. On Monday the old rules of 1948 were bad. On Wednesday the bad old rules and precedents of 1948 were cited by the same people, and now they were good. The rule of seating delegates in 1948 was lamentable on Monday. On Wednesday the precedent of 1948 was invoked to seat delegates, so long as they were for Eisenhower.[6]

So the convention, by a small margin, without hearing any of the evidence, overruled the Credentials Committee, overruled the Republican National Committee, threw out the Taft delegates from Georgia, Texas and Louisiana, and seated Eisenhower delegates.

After the votes were counted on the issue of the contested delegates, it was all over but the shouting. On the first ballot, Eisenhower received 595 votes—nine short of victory. Suddenly Harold Stassen's Minnesota banner waved frantically and swung to Ike the winning bloc of sixteen votes.

In the fall of 1952, Senator Robert A. Taft prepared his own analysis of why he lost the Republican nomination the preceding July. He correctly and forcefully described the reasons as follows:

> First, it was the power of the New York financial interests and a large number of businessmen subject to New York influence. . . . Second, four-fifths of the influential newspapers in the country were opposed to me continuously and vociferously and many turned themselves into propaganda sheets for my opponent.
>
> The making of a moral issue out of the Texas case was only possible because every internationalist paper sent special

> writers to blow up a contest which ordi-
> narily would have been settled fairly by
> the National Committee and the Creden-
> tials Committee. . . . If there had not been
> these issues, the publicity firms would
> have invented others to be shouted by the
> pro-Eisenhower press.[7]

Eisenhower was not responsible for any of the vicious tactics used to win his nomination. Taft did not blame him, and no responsible Republican blames him. He repudiated the illegal tactics used by his managers in Texas.

After the nomination, the Eisenhower managers started to lead Eisenhower through the same empty campaign and meaningless oratory that had charac-terized Willkie and Dewey. Some forthright spokes-men in the Eisenhower camp began publicly to express their concern. The pro-Ike Scripps-Howard newspapers cried out in anguish that Eisenhower's campaign was "running like a dry creek."

As a result, General Eisenhower personally seized control of his campaign and called on Senator Taft for help. On September 12, 1952, they met in New York and issued a campaign document which gave the voters a choice on foreign policy, the first choice in twenty years. This document, called the Morn-ingside Declaration said:

> General Eisenhower will give this country an administration inspired by Republican principles of continued and expanding liberty for all as against the continued growth of New Deal socialism which we would suffer under Governor Stevenson, representative of the left-wingers, if not a left-winger himself.

Speaking in Buffalo, New York, General Eisenhower promised to "clean out the State Department from top to bottom." He approved the campaign slogan: "Corruption, Communism, and Korea." General Eisenhower and all Republican candidates in 1952 campaigned on the Republican Party Platform adopted by the 1952 Convention which promised:

> We shall eliminate from the State Department and from every Federal office, all, wherever they may be found, who share responsibility for the needless predicaments and perils in which we find ourselves. We shall also sever from the public payroll the hoards of loafers, incompetents and unnecessary employees who clutter the administration of our foreign affairs. . . . The Government of the

United States, under Republican leadership, will repudiate all commitments contained in secret understandings such as those of Yalta which aid Communist enslavements. . . .We shall again make liberty into a beacon light of hope that will penetrate the dark places . . . We shall see to it that no treaty or agreement with other countries deprives our citizens of the rights guaranteed them by the Federal Constitution. . . . There are no Communists in the Republican Party . . . We never compromised with Communism and we have fought to expose it and to eliminate it in government and American life. A Republican President will appoint only persons of unquestioned loyalty. . . . Reduction of expenditures by the elimination of waste and extravagance so that the budget will be balanced and a general tax reduction can be made.

To the dismay of the kingmakers, as well as of the liberals and Democrats, the Republican Party closed ranks. Aided by Senator Joseph McCarthy's television analysis of candidate Stevenson's soft-on-communism record, Republicans offered the people the choice they had been denied for four presidential elections. The result is history.

The kingmakers were somewhat nonplused at Eisenhower's victory and its meaning. His election in November was a clear mandate to repudiate the New Deal foreign policy, stop coddling communists, win the war in Korea, end corruption in government, and cut federal spending.

The kingmakers are very resourceful. They moved quietly and efficiently to guarantee that the Republican campaign pledges of 1952 would not be fulfilled. Their task was made easy because Eisenhower was, admittedly, an amateur in politics. He was as out of his depth as Taft would have been as Commander of SHAEF.

Eisenhower did his best and loyally stood by Ezra Taft Benson and Richard Nixon when the kingmakers tried to force them out of his official family. But after eight years, the objective observer has to admit that we still had the same America Last foreign policy, there was no housecleaning in the State Department, we accepted a stalemate instead of victory in Korea, and federal spending was higher than ever.

Moreover, those eight years saw steady deterioration in the strength of the Republican Party. Eisenhower never could transfer his magnetism to other Republican candidates. Eisenhower could not elect a Republican Congress in 1954, 1956 or 1958 and could not elect his handpicked successor, Richard Nixon, running against a little known senator from a small state in 1960.

In 1951, before Eisenhower's election, there were twenty-five Republican governors. In 1959 there were only fourteen. In 1951, there were forty-seven Republican senators and 199 Republican congressmen; in 1959 there were only thirty-four senators and 153 congressmen. In 1951 there were 754 Republican state senators and 2566 Republican state representatives, in 1959 there were only 592 and 1942 respectively. After seven years of President Eisenhower's leadership, the Republicans had lost 24 percent of the vital offices they had held *before* his election.

Taft was one of the first Republicans to wake up to how the kingmakers, after using Eisenhower to win the election, promptly used him as a cover for the perpetuation of the Roosevelt-Truman foreign policy and the failure to fulfill the Republican Platform of 1952. In the White House on April 30, 1953, before a dozen congressmen and others, Taft told President Eisenhower:

> You're taking us right down the same road
> that Truman traveled. It's a repudiation
> of everything we promised in the [1952]
> campaign.

As the years passed, most of those who had stolen the Republican nomination for Eisenhower departed involuntarily from the political scene. In the same election that Eisenhower won, Senator Henry Cabot Lodge was defeated for reelection by John F. Kennedy. Sherman Adams, Ike's chief administrative assistant, had to beat a hasty retreat from public life after revelations that he had accepted a vicuna coat and a Turkish rug for interceding for Bernard Goldfine. Oveta Culp Hobby resigned as Secretary of Health, Education and Welfare, after her department had to take responsibility for the costly premature licensing of the Salk polio vaccine. Herbert Brownell resigned as attorney general after legal scholars pointed out that he gave President Eisenhower bad advice on Little Rock and should have used marshals instead of federal soldiers.[8] Donald Eastvold, attorney general of the state of Washington, who was the star speaker for the kingmakers on the issue of the contested delegates, warning the delegates of the grave moral turpitude they would commit if they seated Taft's southern delegates, abandoned his political career and left his own state. Paul Hoffman, one of those who had persuaded Eisenhower to enter politics, failed in his efforts to keep the American Studebaker plants operating and finally married a prominent liberal Democrat, Anna Rosenberg. Harold Stassen has since sustained a steady succession of lopsided defeats in the primaries, proving that his kingmaker support was not shared by the voters.

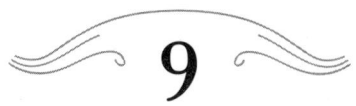

9

Here Comes That Man Again

1956

As the Republican Convention of 1956 approached, the renomination of President Eisenhower was a foregone conclusion. There was a little flurry about Ike's heart attack, but the pros never considered the possibility of running any other candidate. Republicans looked forward to a joyful convention in San Francisco.

The uncertainty about Eisenhower's physical condition, however, did give the kingmakers serious concern about the vice presidential nominee. The kingmakers had accepted Richard Nixon in 1952 because he had helped to deliver the California delegation to the Eisenhower faction on the first crucial issues.

But the kingmakers never really trusted Nixon for two reasons: (1) he was not a creature of their own making, therefore he was not beholden to them; and (2) he had risen to fame as an anti-communist investigator, as one of those chiefly responsible for the prosecution of Alger Hiss. For this, the Democrats hated him with the unreasoning partisan reaction that caused Harry Truman to call the Hiss case "a red herring"; the Liberal Establishment would never forgive him; and the secret kingmakers were afraid of him because they consistently oppose raising either the domestic or foreign issue of communism. They fear that it will open a Pandora's Box of public reaction which might bring about a change in the America Last pro-communist foreign policy in which they have a vested interest.

With the reins of the presidency held only by the strings of Ike's injured heart, the kingmakers decided to dump Nixon from the Republican ticket.

The kingmakers whistled, and again came forth their faithful friend and ally, Harold Stassen, who was at the time Special Assistant for Disarmament Policy, a position that gave him Cabinet status. At a formal news conference on July 23, 1956, Stassen announced his support of Governor Christian A. Herter of Massachusetts, calling him "6%" stronger than Nixon as a vice-presidential candidate. Stassen was granted a four-week leave of absence from the Eisenhower administration to pursue his campaign to persuade the Republicans to drop Nixon.[1]

To the general public, this appeared to be a one-man crusade that spontaneously picked up momentum as Stassen issued each new statement. To the discerning observer, however, there was more to this tactic than met the eye. There was behind-the-scenes support in very high places. There was mysterious financial support. In the background were a number of powerful but shadowy figures. One of these was identified by the Chief of the UPI Washington bureau as General Lucius Clay.[2]

The key to this maneuver was the choice of Christian Herter. Why was he, of all Republicans, selected? Herter was a man with no particular talent or national following. He was a poor public speaker and, since he was badly crippled by arthritis, he was even less physically vigorous than Eisenhower after his heart attack.

Herter was picked because he was a reliable ally of the kingmakers and the foreign policy they sought to preserve. As a congressman from Massachusetts, he had sponsored in the House of Representatives the foreign aid bill which became known as the Marshall Plan, which proved to be so financially profitable to the kingmakers. He had helped to organize the Council on Foreign Relations which has been the chief sponsor of the disastrous America Last foreign policy.

When the kingmakers discovered that Nixon was so strong with organization Republicans that they could not dump him without endangering Ike's own reelection, they gave up and Herter made the nominating speech for Nixon. When Herter completed his tedious speech at the Cow Palace, the delegates breathed a sigh of relief that one so lacking in popular appeal was not their vice presidential candidate.

Christian A. Herter was rewarded for his part in the dump-Nixon move by being named Under Secretary of State. When John Foster Dulles died, Herter was advanced to Secretary of State, a post for which he had no known qualifications—except that he had been cleared by the kingmakers as a certified sponsor of huge foreign handouts.

Herter presided over the worst blunder in the 100-year history of the Republican Party. It was under Herter that the U.S. State Department, ignoring the reports from our ambassadors to Cuba, assisted Castro to power.

10

Surrender in Manhattan

1960

I mmediately after Eisenhower and Nixon were reelected in 1956, the secret kingmakers realized that Richard Nixon would be the front-runner at the 1960 Convention. They laid their plans early and carefully.

This time their candidate was Nelson Rockefeller, whose political career had been nourished at just the right speed as governor of New York, and whose image had been carefully built by a full-fledged image-making organization with a staff of seventy persons comprising six divisions with separate functions.

Rockefeller jumped with both feet into the 1960 race, and ran hard. Rockefeller's campaign was noteworthy for the way he removed himself from the "mainstream" of Republican policy by opposing the

Eisenhower-Nixon position and agreeing with the Democrat position on such key issues as the mythical "missile gap," the U-2 incident, and medicare.

A few weeks before the Republican Convention was to open in Chicago, the kingmakers surveyed the situation. They faced the hard reality that Nixon had carefully built his political fences within the Republican Party for many years, his organization support was solid, and he would be difficult if not impossible to defeat for the nomination.

The New York kingmakers are resourceful and persistent. They decided that, if they couldn't beat him, they would try to influence him. They fell back on the tactic they had tried with Senator Taft at the Ogden Reid dinner in June of 1940.

And so it came to pass that, on the Saturday before the Republican Convention opened in Chicago, Nixon made a pilgrimage to New York where he met for eight hours at Rockefeller's Fifth Avenue apartment. At the conclusion of that meeting, Nixon agreed to accept the changes in the Republican Platform that Rockefeller demanded.

The Republican Platform Committee had been meeting in Chicago for an entire week, laboriously pounding out the platform which would reflect the views of Republicans from all the fifty states. Now the Platform Committee was handed the Rocke-feller-Nixon orders: Throw out your week's work, the money and time you have spent at your own expense to come to Chicago and hear witnesses and draft a document to submit to the convention, throw it all out and accept the Rockefeller-Nixon Platform worked out in secret 700 miles from the convention.

Republicans everywhere understood the meaning and significance of the new Rockefeller-Nixon alliance. It meant much more than mere changes of words in the platform. It meant that Nixon had paid the price that Taft had been unwilling to pay. He had purged himself of his independence and made himself acceptable to the New York kingmakers. Rank and file Republicans knew that this forbode a turn toward the same "liberal me-tooism" which had twice defeated Dewey.

Senator Barry Goldwater promptly labelled the new Nixon alliance a "surrender to Rockefeller."[1] Goldwater said the entire convention had been the victim of an "unprecedented last-minute attempt" to impose a platform dictated by "a spokesman for the ultra-liberals." Goldwater interpreted Nixon's mission to New York as "paying court on the leader of the Republican left," and as "a bid to appease the Republican left."

Goldwater continued with a statement that was remarkable both for its candor and its prophetic nature. He said: "I believe this to be immoral politics.

I also believe it to be self-defeating." He predicted that the Rockefeller-Nixon agreement will "live in history as the Munich of the Republican Party" and will guarantee "a Republican defeat in November."

As his part of the bargain, Rockefeller made a seconding speech for Nixon at the convention. To the bewilderment of the television audience, Rockefeller nominated "Richard E. (for Milhous) Nixon." A Rockefeller intimate later explained this mistake: "Rocky imagined he was nominating Thomas E. Dewey."

Nixon confirmed his new alliance by accepting as his running mate one of the darlings of the internationalist clique, one of the discredited hatchet men of the smear-Taft maneuver in 1952, and also of the get-McCarthy cabal of 1954, Henry Cabot Lodge.

Newspaper reporter Edward Lindsay summed up the surrender like this:

> The Republican Party now stands not only left of the late Senator Robert A. Taft, but somewhat pointedly left of President Eisenhower.[2]

The result of Nixon's surrender was that, like Willkie and Dewey before him, Nixon pulled his punches and failed to campaign on the fundamental issues. He beat a steady retreat from the conservative and anti-communist principles which alone could bring victory for Republicans. Nixon's surrender to Rockefeller was not productive; Rockefeller failed to carry his own state for Nixon.

Republicans should remember that the kingmakers are quite willing to have their candidate talk like a real Republican when seeking the nomination. But once he is nominated, then a Dr. Jekyll and Mr. Hyde transformation takes place, and he switches from a fiery fighter to a milk-toast "me too" candidate. Kingmaker candidates are brainwashed into acting like they would rather be anti-right than be president.

Henry Cabot Lodge's campaign disappointed even the liberals. According to *Newsweek*, "His laziness became legend. The Lodge entourage started the day late and shut up shop early. He canceled an upstate New York visit to take his wife to Niagara Falls on the Canadian side." He canceled five of seven appearances in Kansas City in order to watch TV.[3]

After the 1960 election, it was not hindsight, but sorrow that his foresight had proved so accurate, when Senator Goldwater said the Nixon-Lodge ticket lost "not because we were Republicans but because we were not Republican enough." Goldwater analyzed what happened to rank-and-file Republicans during the 1960 campaign like this:

> Eighty per cent of the delegates to the Republican National Convention in 1960 were Conservatives. They felt let down by the platform. . . . In the campaign, they became disenchanted; Nixon appeared to be just another me-too candidate . . . These people do not feel that their concept of Republicanism is being reflected at the leadership level.[4]

And the kingmakers? Did they shed any tears when Nixon and Lodge lost? Oh no; they were not unhappy at all. They never liked Nixon very much anyway, and Lodge always was considered expendable. The kingmakers breathed a sigh of relief, secure in the knowledge that Nixon was shelved, and the America Last foreign policy would continue under Kennedy and Johnson and their coterie of ADA advisers.

11

The Obvious Choice

1964

By mid-1963, impartial observers could see that the Republican Party had one obvious, logical, deserving, winning candidate. He combined the integrity of Robert A. Taft with the glamour of Dwight Eisenhower. He had proved his ability to win against heavy odds. He was truly *a national* candidate with a demonstrated following in all the fifty states. For the first time, Republicans had a candidate with genuine appeal to the youth of America. When Senator Barry Goldwater at long last announced he would be a candidate, this was in response to a genuine grassroots movement—not the result of a publicity blitz.

This obvious candidate had been a success at everything he has tried. Like Eisenhower, this obvious candidate is a General, and like Taft he has vast political experience. He is the epitome of American constitutional principles.

He was a successful businessman. He is a successful author; his two books were best-sellers: *The Conscience of a Conservative* and *Why Not Victory?* He had a distinguished World War II record; he has risen to the rank of Major General in the Air Force Reserve, and he still pilots jet fighter planes, a remarkable feat for one of his age and position.

He has been a tremendous success in politics. He was twice elected Senator from Arizona, a state where the Democratic registrations outnumber Republicans two to one. He successfully held one of the most important jobs in the Republican Party: Chairman of the Republican Senatorial Campaign Committee. He is the most sought-after speaker in the United States today.

The obvious nominee of the Republican Party in 1964 was Senator Barry Goldwater.

Goldwater has the magic quality of leadership that is based on independence of thought and courage. An almost-forgotten incident in his legislative career proves how the Goldwater brand of leadership can prevail even when a minority of one.

In 1959 the Senate passed what was popularly known as the Kennedy "sweetheart" labor bill by the staggering margin of ninety to one. Senator

Goldwater was the lone dissenter. He voted against the bill on the ground that it allowed Senator Kennedy, a presidential aspirant, to give the appearance of sponsoring labor reform legislation; whereas, his bill could be properly described as like a flea bite on the hide of a bull elephant. The entire press predicted that Senator Goldwater's dissent was a futile gesture and that the Kennedy bill would pass the House quickly and become law.

Then a remarkable thing happened. Because of the brilliant way that Senator Goldwater had focused attention on the issue of monopoly versus freedom, our Congressmen began to hear from their constituents back home.

As a result, it was not the Kennedy "sweetheart" bill, but a real labor reform bill called the Landrum-Griffin Act, which passed the House and ultimately became law as a substitute for the Kennedy bill.

Senator Goldwater gave us dramatic proof that conservatism is popular. He showed that a minority of one can ultimately be victorious against overwhelming odds.

Any political leader can score a win if he has the votes in his pocket, just as any general can win if he has more men and more weapons. The true test of leadership is the ability to carry your side to victory when the odds are against you. This is the kind of leadership Barry Goldwater has demonstrated in a political way in Arizona, and in a legislative way in the Senate.

This is leadership that can win elections and solve problems at home, and defeat the Communists abroad. This is the leadership for which America yearns today.

Most important, Barry Goldwater is the one Republican who can and will win—because he will campaign on the issues of 1964. He is the one Republican who will not pull his punches to please the kingmakers. He can be counted on to face the issues squarely. He will make the kind of forthright hard-hitting campaign that American voters admire. This is why he is the man the left-leaning liberals most fear. He is the only Republican who will truly offer the voters "a choice, not an echo."

As Goldwater's grassroots strength grew in 1963 and early 1964, the leftwing propaganda against him grew in geometric proportion. *Life* magazine put into words an anti-Goldwater argument that has appeared in one form or another in numerous magazines and newspaper columns. *Life* said we must beware of Goldwater because he has one-sentence solutions for national problems. According to this peculiar line of egghead reasoning, present day problems are so complex that we must have sophisticated—not simple—solutions.

Contrary to this argument, civilization progresses, freedom is won, and problems are solved because we have wonderful people who think up simple solutions! It is not the complicated, roundabout Rube Goldberg approach that accomplishes anything, but the direct approach that goes to the heart of the problem.

The man who did as much as anyone to emancipate women from their daily drudgery was the inventor of the sewing machine. His invention depended on a very simple idea; just put the eye of the needle in the point instead of in the other end.

Two brothers named Wright who ran a bicycle shop in Dayton, Ohio, had the ambition to invent an airplane. They received long letters from experts at the Smithsonian Institution and from professors at European universities telling them that heavier-than-air flight was impossible. But the Wright brothers had two simple solutions—the curved wing to provide lift, and the propeller—and with these simple solutions, they built and flew the first airplane. Their simple solutions dominated air travel until the perfection of the jet engine.

When our infant Republic was threatened by the greatest military conquerer of the 19th century, our Minister to France said: "Millions for defense sir, but not one cent for tribute." This simple solution brought peace, not war.

When an American citizen named Perdicaris was captured and held hostage by a bandit named Raisuli, President Theodore Roosevelt had a simple solution: just send a cable reading "Perdicaris alive or Raisuli dead." It got results; Perdicaris was promptly released. Today, American servicemen are held hostage by Red bandits from East Germany to Cuba, to Red China, and no one has tried to get them out by simple solutions.

In 1958 the Chinese Reds made their big drive to take over Quemoy and Matsu. Appeasement-minded pundits at home urged that we evacuate these islands because "Why die for Quemoy?" President Eisenhower had a simple solution: he just went on television and told the world the United States would stand firm in the Formosa Straits. Shortly afterwards the Reds gave up their attacks, and for six years these islands have been secure outposts of freedom.

Likewise, there are numerous simple solutions for most of the problems that confront our country today. Barry Goldwater is the man who can cut through the egghead complexities in Foggy Bottom and solve these problems for us.

There is a very simple solution for what to do about Cuba—just reinstate the Monroe Doctrine. It would rid us of Castro and his subversion. We should not submit to the international blackmail of the false claim that using the Monroe Doctrine will start World War III. In 140 years of use, the Monroe Doctrine never brought war; it brought only peace. It would bring peace today if only we had a president with the courage to use it. Barry Goldwater is that man.

There was a very simple solution to what to do about the Berlin Wall. The Soviets started building it on Friday evening after our president had left Washington for a weekend holiday. By the time he returned to the White House on Monday afternoon, the Wall was built; the State Department wrung its hands and said: "There is nothing we can do now. What do you want to do, start World War III?" The solution was simple. A president with leadership could have made this announcement Friday night: "If the communists close that door in Berlin, we will close the doors of the Soviet Embassy and consulates in our country." The Soviets would do anything to keep open these privileged sanctuaries which serve as the headquarters of their subversion, espionage and propaganda in the United States.

There was a very simple solution to what to do about the Congo: let the Congolese solve it! When they had a chance, they got rid of the communist Lumumba. They would have eliminated the rest of the communists, if our State Department had not, in collusion with the UN, told the Congolese they had to be more democratic and admit communist followers of Lumumba into their government.

There is a simple solution as to what to do about Southeast Asia: just follow the advice of our greatest military authority on the Far East, General Douglas MacArthur. He said that Red China's aggressions could be stopped by announcing the end of the privileged Red sanctuaries requested by Attlee, granted by Acheson and still respected. General MacArthur thought it was wrong to send American boys to die in Asia, while refusing to use any of the 600,000 trained soldiers of the Republic of China or other means available for victory.

There is a very simple solution to what to do about the problem of world communism: just stop helping the communists. The Soviet empire would die of its own economic anemia if Democratic administrations didn't keep giving it massive blood transfusions, such as the sending of sixty-four million bushels of American wheat.

There is a very simple solution to the problem of peace and disarmament. It was given to us by the father of our country, George Washington. The formula is as good today as when he said it: "If we desire to secure peace . . . it must be known that we are at all times ready for war."

Finally, there is a very simple solution to what to do about the whole "looney" mess in Washington today—elect Barry Goldwater, the man with the courage to give us simple solutions.

12

Anybody but Goldwater

After Barry Goldwater announced his candidacy, the big question was: Where did the secret kingmakers fit into the 1964 picture? Would they say: "We picked the Republican nominee at each of the last seven conventions, so it is only fair to let someone else have a chance?" Would the kingmakers concede: "We had New Yorker Wendell Willkie in 1940, New Yorker Tom Dewey in 1944 and 1948, New Yorker Dwight Eisenhower in 1952 and 1956, and Richard Nixon who is now a New Yorker in 1960—and it is time for one of the other forty-nine states to name the nominee?" Would the kingmakers admit: "Goldwater is the obvious choice, so we'll sit this one out?"

Anyone who thought these things was quickly brought to reality in 1964. The kingmakers recognized

Goldwater as a Republican they could not control. They started from the premise that the Republican Convention must nominate *anybody* but Goldwater.

The chief propaganda organ of the secret king-makers, the *New York Times,* revealed this drive for anybody but Goldwater in a surprisingly candid article bylined by one of its Washington correspondents, Tom Wicker. This report said:

> The most bitter resistance to Senator Goldwater centers in the "eastern, internationalist power structure that for two decades has dictated Republican nominations. The members of that elite will not lightly relinquish their party to Barry Goldwater."[1]

Popular national magazines goosestepped for this "internationalist power structure" by featuring anti-Goldwater articles. The November 2, 1963 issue of the *New Yorker,* a slick sophisticated magazine beamed to the carriage trade, sandwiched a profile on Goldwater amid 200 pages of luxury advertising. The author was Richard Rovere, a former editor of the communist magazine *New Masses*. *Newsweek* magazine of November 4, 1963, featured a byline column called "The Odds Against Goldwater" by Emmet John Hughes, who turned out a neat, but false, phrase, and said that Goldwater would not win because "he had yet—seriously—to face his foes . . . to face his friends . . . to face the issues." The fact is that no politician in either party has made his position as clear as has Goldwater, who has written two books defining his position on all major issues.

The *Saturday Evening Post* of January 25, 1964, featured an article called "How the Republicans Can Win" by Arthur Larson, the originator of the term "modern Republicanism." Larson, who never won an election, advised the GOP that it could win only if it appealed to the "Authentic American Center." When he proceeded to define where this is, the only recent prominent figure he could think of who occupied the "Center" was President Kennedy who, like President Johnson, was recorded as voting conservative on only 10 percent of his Senate votes.

Behind the scenes, the kingmakers prepared the publicity buildup of several candidates to replace Barry Goldwater. How can the average person spot the kingmakers' candidates? Here is a sure litmus-paper test:

1. A kingmaker candidate does not criticize other kingmaker candidates.
2. Kingmaker candidates criticize Senator Goldwater more than they criticize Lyndon Johnson.

3. Kingmaker candidates never criticize the Democratic foreign giveaway programs.
4. Kingmaker candidates never criticize the State Department or the concessions it has made to the communist axis.
5. Kingmaker candidates hardly ever raise the issue of communism, either foreign or domestic.

The first choice of the kingmakers was Nelson Rockefeller. Who else but Nels? But Rockefeller chose a second wife rather than a second chance at the presidency. He remained in the race on the off-hand chance that he might, by some stroke of luck, win the crown; but primarily his function was to be a "spoiler." The kingmakers used Rockefeller to make a direct attack on Goldwater, so that, as we went into the stretch, the word could be passed down from on high that "Goldwater and Rockefeller have both made so many enemies that what we need is a compromise candidate who will be acceptable to both sides."

Rockefeller candidly admitted that when he was "the frontrunner, as I was, it's natural to try to unite all wings of the party," but after Goldwater forged ahead, "I'm off the unity kick." His name-calling blasts at Goldwater included such intemperate language as "ruthless, roughshod intimidation . . . cynical expediency . . . betrayal of principles."[2]

The second prong of the assault against Goldwater was to encourage state delegations pledged to favorite sons so that deals could be made at the opportune moment. Meanwhile the kingmakers engaged in a frantic search to dig up anybody—just anybody—to prevent Republicans from selecting their obvious candidate.

About once a month, some spokesman for the kingmakers sent up a trial balloon to test public reaction to a new candidate. In 1963 a trial balloon was sent up for General Lauris Norstad. He is very handsome and has a fine head of hair which, while Kennedy was President, seemed to be important qualifications.

Next came a boomlet for George Romney, Governor of Michigan. Like Rockefeller, and unlike Goldwater or Lyndon Johnson, Romney is handicapped by the absence of World War II military service. Even after he was dropped by the kingmakers, Romney was faithful to their wishes. On June 7, he violated his long standing rule against politicking on Sunday to announce: "I will do everything within my power to prevent him (Goldwater) from becoming the party's presidential choice."

One day in early 1964, a reporter asked Richard Nixon who he thought the next Republican nominee would be. Nixon replied that there were three

strong candidates: Nelson Rockefeller, Barry Goldwater and Lucius Clay. The inclusion of Lucius Clay
came as quite a surprise to rank-and-file Republicans. Why did Lucius Clay rate mention as one of
the three top candidates? Clay is one of the inner
clique of secret kingmakers, and Nixon, allowing
himself to be used as a spokesman, was sending up
a trial balloon.

As the convention approached, the kingmakers
had almost exhausted their list of "stop Goldwater" candidates: Harold Stassen, who hasn't been
elected in more than 20 years; Henry Cabot Lodge,
Lyndon Johnson's Ambassador to South Vietnam,
who was last elected to office in 1946, and who
has since suffered two major defeats; and Richard
Nixon, who abandoned California after his defeat
for governor and moved into an apartment building in New York owned and occupied by Nelson
Rockefeller.

The kingmakers realized the crucial nature of
the California primary on June 2 and threw their
vast financial and propaganda apparatus behind
Nelson Rockefeller. The San Francisco and Los
Angeles newspapers, *Look*, *Newsweek*, *Time* and
Life magazines, the columnists and commentators,
the pollsters, etc., all attacked Goldwater in every
conceivable manner. Goldwater's victory proved
that even a fortune in paid workers and hidden

persuaders could not match the tens of thousands of dedicated volunteer grassroots workers who didn't stop until the ballots were counted.

Remaining after California was only William W. Scranton, Governor of Pennsylvania. Until the stimulated publicity started in early 1964, Scranton was unknown in national affairs. His entire political experience consisted of one term in the House of Representatives and one year as governor.

Four different groups of well-placed individuals in Harrisburg, in Philadelphia, in New York, and elsewhere in the Northeast had worked individually and in concert to promote Scranton as a presidential candidate. While the average citizen could detect no formal coordination among them, there was no working at cross-purposes, and they all acted with Scranton's knowledge. Here are the four developments.[3]

In Philadelphia, the kingmakers conducted a careful project of "exposure"—showing off Scranton to leading banking, industrial and communications figures in a series of private luncheons. The current representative of the Morgan Guaranty Trust Company of New York is its president, Thomas S. Gates, former secretary of defense. Gates of Morgan Guaranty is the kingmaker successor of Thomas Lamont of J. P. Morgan and Company who masterminded the Willkie blitz.

The host of these exclusive luncheons was Thomas B. McCabe, president of Scott Paper Company and, more importantly, former chairman of the Board of Governors of the Federal Reserve System and Public Governor of the New York Stock Exchange.

The McCabe luncheons exposed Governor Scranton both to potential big money contributors and to key individuals in the communications field. Among the key industrialists and news media persuaders who attended these luncheons were former Secretary of Defense Neil McElroy, now chairman of the Procter and Gamble soap empire; Walter Thayer, former counsel of the Citizens for Eisenhower and now president of the *New York Herald Tribune*; Arthur H. Dean, senior partner in the largest New York law firm, Sullivan and Cromwell; David Kendall, former White House counsel, now a Chrysler corporation vice president; and James Hagerty, Eisenhower's press secretary and now an American Broadcasting Company vice president, in which capacity he defended the television attack on Richard Nixon by Alger Hiss on Veteran's Day, 1962.

The money and publicity potential of these luncheons was more than adequate to launch Scranton full-blown as a presidential candidate. The guest list at these luncheons included many of the important financial contacts McCabe has made in forty-seven years as a businessman and banker, all potential contributors when the time became ripe. Thomas S. Gates had also helped lay the financial groundwork with his important contractors and with bankers and businessmen in Philadelphia and New York. Scranton himself has an estimated $9,000,000 fortune, enough to make a considerable contribution to the pre-convention effort.

In Harrisburg, Scranton's hand-picked Republican state chairman, Craig Truax, and other Pennsylvania Republican officials worked to soft-sell out-of-state Republicans on Scranton as the man who could bind up the GOP wounds expected from the Rockefeller-Goldwater pre-convention battle. Truax suggested to Goldwater supporters in the south and elsewhere that Scranton would be their best alternative if Goldwater did not get the nomination.

In New York, a young lawyer named Warren J. Sinsheimer launched a "Draft Scranton" campaign in the pattern of the popular petition effort for Wendell Willkie in 1940. Sinsheimer conferred with close Scranton political confidants and, while he was given no official approval, neither was he told to stop.

It is significant that Draft Scranton petitions carried the following wording at the top:

> The undersigned urge Governor William
> Scranton of Pennsylvania to seek actively
> the 1964 Republican Presidential Nomi-
> nation. *Regardless of political affiliation*,
> we the undersigned urge that he be nom-
> inated for President at the Republican
> National Convention. (emphasis added)[4]

In other words, as in 1940 and especially in 1952, the kingmakers urged non-Republicans to come over and help prevent the Republican National Convention from nominating its obvious first choice.

In the communications media, the publicity blitz was given the GO signal. As one newspaperman put it, suddenly "Governor Scranton has become hot copy." National reporters began running in and out of Harrisburg at an unprecedented pace, and competing news organizations scrambled to keep pace. The *New York Herald Tribune* led off with an editorial titled "Calling Governor Scranton." Stewart Alsop, an ADA founder, was the author of a feature article in the *Saturday Evening Post* called "The Logical Candidate." The *New York Times Magazine* gave large space to favorable portrayals of Scranton. The *Wall Street Journal* joined the cabal and called Scranton "the betting favorite among some of the most knowledgeable GOP leaders." Walter Lippmann advised Republicans to nominate Scranton even though conceding that Scranton had little prospect of defeating Johnson.

Scranton was the subject of a friendly cover story in *Newsweek*. *Look* had a flattering article and the *Reader's Digest* joined in with six pages of fulsome praise. Scranton was featured in *Fortune* in a long story about his state industrial development. *Life* magazine highlighted a lengthy profile by Theodore H. White, author of the prize-winning book about President Kennedy. The Luce publications have always been part of the kingmaking establishment. It certainly is no handicap to Scranton that his brother-in-law, James A. Linen, is President of *Time*.

The *St. Louis Globe-Democrat* predicted that when all these developments are

> pulled together and coordinated by men
> who know how nominees are made, they
> provide all the basic ingredients—money
> publicity, party support, seasoned political
> leadership and popular grass roots activ-
> ity—to make a presidential candidate.[5]

After saying he would accept only a "genuine draft that is not engineered"—which never developed—Scranton drafted himself just one month before the Convention opened.

13

Victory for the Grassroots

1964

G overnor Scranton started on the campaign trail by announcing that his hope of winning the nomination lay in taking some 200 "moveable" delegates from Barry Goldwater's announced pledges of more than 600. Immediately the kingmakers' immense financial and propaganda apparatus went into high gear to sell Scranton to Republicans. His every ghost-written word became front-page copy, with ghostwriters Malcolm Moos and William Keisling scripting Goldwater as the villain instead of LBJ. The other kingmaker candidates closed ranks behind Scranton; Henry Cabot Lodge rushed home from South Vietnam to jump on the Scranton bandwagon. As the kingmakers twisted the arm of our communications media,

Scranton began a meteoric rise on that adjustable thermometer of kingmaker hopes, the Gallup Poll.

As the delegates gathered in San Francisco for the 1964 Republican National Convention, the kingmakers trotted out all their tried-and-true tactics of previous conventions. A veteran journalist, personally opposed to Goldwater and writing for an anti-Goldwater newspaper, described this onslaught:

> An attack upon Goldwater of a ferocity never remotely approached in any of the eight national party conventions previously attended by this columnist was then opened . . . They, the "moderns," loosed upon Goldwater a storm of accusation and innuendo that made their assaults upon the late Senator Robert A. Taft in 1952 look like warm endorsements. Men of the stature of Nelson Rockefeller and Henry Cabot Lodge appeared before 40,000 Negro demonstrators in the streets in open incitation of them against the candidacy of the man about to be chosen to head their own party, Goldwater.

Scranton camp followers spread shocking tales suggesting that Goldwater was perhaps in league with neo-Nazis in

Germany—and this about a man whose own father was Jewish. Scranton himself attacked Goldwater, in his challenge to a "debate," in tones plainly implying that Goldwater was not only wrong but actually evil.[1]

These tactics were not successful, because in 1964 the majority of convention delegates were independent citizens elected in their districts who sought not personal advancement or political jobs but only the nomination and election of a candidate who would end the America Last policies of the past thirty years.

On July 12 the kingmakers released their contrived Gallup and Harris polls. The latter falsely described the Goldwater position as favoring "Go to war over Cuba," "Using A-bombs in Asia," and "Against social security." The unscientific nature of many polls was revealed by Marvin D. Field, formerly with the Gallup poll and now head of one of the polls which picked Rockefeller to beat Goldwater in the California primary, who admitted to the press that he polled only 256 out of 3,002,038 registered Republicans in California. He thus based his prediction on .000085 of Republican voters.[2]

As a result of a luncheon strategy conference on July 12 with Rockefeller and Lodge, Scranton caused to be drafted and released that evening his letter which charged that Goldwater had "bought, beaten and compromised" the delegates. This was a revealing admission from the kingmakers that they thought the 1964 Republican delegates could be "bought" and "compromised."

As the convention opened on July 13, the final strategy of the kingmakers was to harass and delay the convention by raising phony issues in the hope that a miracle would happen. Each day Henry Cabot Lodge (referred to at the Cow Palace as Henry Sabotage) announced we could expect a "surprise" or a "bombshell." The kingmaker forces waged a tedious struggle in the Rules Committee and also in the Credentials Committee where they tried to raise the spurious issues of race, but were able to muster only 19 votes out of 100.

On July 14 Nelson Rockefeller and George Romney demanded that the Republican Platform be amended to include an anti-extremism plank. They denounced some Goldwater supporters as extremists, but were unwilling to denounce such radical societies as Cosa Nostra, the Black Muslims, CORE (which was then engaged in civil disobedience and lie-ins at the Cow Palace), the Fair Play for Cuba Committee (one of whose members assassinated President Kennedy), the hundreds of Communist fronts on the Attorney General's list; or radical leftwing societies influential in the Democratic Party such as the Americans for Democratic Action and the Ad Hoc Committee for the Triple Revolution. The hypocrisy of these amendments was clear to the delegates who overwhelmingly voted them down.

Rockefeller complained that his speech was interrupted by the delegates. As long as he confined himself to the subject, he was given quiet attention. But the California delegates knew he had conducted a rough no-holds-barred campaign against Goldwater in their state and had mailed out a million reprints of *Look* Magazine's smear on Goldwater. When Rockefeller insinuated that Goldwater supporters used "Communist and Nazi methods" and cited the cancellation of his political appearance at a University in Los Angeles (Loyola, for reasons it considered proper), the California delegates voiced disapproval of his smear. As John L. Lewis said in explaining his fisticuffs with Bill Hutcheson at an AFL Convention, when an honorable man is called a bad name, he must either pretend he didn't hear, or express righteous indignation. California heard because it was the closest delegation to Rocky's rostrum.

The next ploy of the kingmakers was to demand a platform amendment that the president alone should be able to decide on the use of atomic weapons. This was asking the delegates to deny a Republican president the power of deputizing use of atomic weapons which Republicans had entrusted to Democrats Kennedy and Johnson. If, as in 1919 and 1955, the president were stricken for months by a severe heart attack, no one would be authorized to defend our country with nuclear weapons. This kingmaker stratagem was defeated two to one.

The communications media overdid itself in carrying out the directives of the kingmakers to attack Goldwater. On July 16 Senator Goldwater said: "Newspapers like the *New York Times* have to stoop to utter dishonesty in reflecting my views. Some of the newspapers here in San Francisco like the *Chronicle* . . . are nothing but out and out lies." He said a CBS broadcast by Daniel Schorr stating that Goldwater was going to Munich to start his campaign where the fuehrer (Hitler) started his campaign was a "dirty lie."[3] Even the mild-mannered Dwight Eisenhower advised the delegates:

> Let us particularly scorn the divisive efforts of those outside our family, including sensation-seeking columnists and commentators, because, my friends, these are people who couldn't care less about the good of our party.

Republicans will be foolishly naive if they think the defeated kingmakers will now give Goldwater the same party loyalty that conservatives have given them for the past twenty-eight years. While some may give lip service to Goldwater's campaign, realism requires us to anticipate that the kingmakers will use their immense financial and propaganda apparatus in behalf of the reelection of Lyndon Johnson.

Time magazine laid down the line on May 22: "A lot of the kingmakers think that President Johnson, all things being relative, has done a good job." Walter Lippmann expanded on this when he said on May 26 that "the old established ruling powers in the Republican Party—the banking, industrial, and publishing magnates in the large metropolitan centers—are either in favor of the election of President Johnson or at least are not strongly opposed to it." Henry Ford II, who never before voted for any Democrat for president, announced that he would support and vote for President Johnson in the 1964 election because "he's terrific" and "an awful lot of business people are for President Johnson."[4]

14

Who Are the Secret Kingmakers?

everal questions naturally arise: Can it really be possible that a little clique of powerful men meet secretly and plan events that appear to "just happen"? Who are the secret kingmakers who manipulated and controlled Republican National Conventions from 1936 through 1960? What is their motive for exercising such control, even when it means the defeat of the party they profess to serve? These are questions to be answered in this chapter.

The rational citizen believes in the principle of causality, that for every effect there must be a cause. Most of what is ascribed to "accident" or "coincidence" is really the result of human plans. When there is an airplane accident, the authorities make a diligent search for the series of events that led to the crash—and usually the cause is found.

Abraham Lincoln explained causal relationship in his "House Divided" speech:

> But when we see a lot of framed timber, different portions of which we know have been gotten out at different times and places and by different workmen ... and when we see these timbers joined together, and see they exactly make the frame of a house or a mill, all the tenons and mortises exactly fitting, . . . in such a case, we find it impossible not to believe that . . . all understood one another from the beginning, and all worked upon a common plan.

Several years ago, the author of this book stumbled on clear evidence that very powerful men actually do meet to make plans which are kept secret from American citizens. While visiting at Sea Island, Georgia, this writer discovered the details of a secret meeting on nearby St. Simon's Island, Georgia, held at the King and Prince Hotel, February 14–18, 1957.

The most elaborate precautions were taken to prevent Americans from knowing who attended this secret meeting or what transpired there. Advance agents came in four months ahead to check security and search every room in the hotel. All hotel employees were given the most rigid security check and their names sent to Washington for additional investigation. During the four days and five nights of the meeting, all roads leading to the hotel were blocked off and the road block maintained by the Georgia State Police. The hotel was closed to all other patrons. NATO and FBI guards in plain clothes kept constant surveillance on the hotel itself.

None of the hotel employees was permitted to go into the ballroom where the meetings were held. At the end of each session, one of the participants personally gathered up all notes and memos used during the meeting and burned them.

Who were the participants at this secret meeting at St. Simon's Island? They were many of the top-level kingmakers who exercise financial, political and propaganda control over American citizens and policies. The sixty-nine participants on the official unpublished list included the following:

George W. Ball, now Undersecretary of State in the Johnson Administration,

Eugene R. Black, then President of the International Bank for Reconstruction and Development,

McGeorge Bundy, now top presidential adviser on security in the Johnson Administration,

Arthur H. Dean, disarmament negotiator for the State Department under Republican and Democrat administrations,

Thomas E. Dewey, twice Republican presidential candidate,

J. William Fulbright, Senator from Arkansas, later author of the Fulbright Memorandum, a directive to muzzle our military, who on March 25, 1964 called on the United States to "accept Red Cuba,"

Paul G. Hoffman, former U.S. Chief of all foreign aid,

C. D. Jackson, vice president of *Time*, Inc.,

Per Jacobsen, Managing Director, World Monetary Fund,

George F. Kennan, Ambassador to the Soviet Union, and later chief advisor on Communism to the Kennedy Administration,

Henry A. Kissinger, Harvard Professor, director of a Special Studies Project for the Rockefeller Brothers Foundation,

Ralph E. McGill, Editor, *Atlanta Constitution*,

Paul H. Nitze, later Secretary of the Navy in the Johnson Administration,

David Rockefeller, now president of the Chase Manhattan Bank,

Dean Rusk, now Secretary of State,

Arthur Hays Sulzberger, president and publisher of the *New York Times*,

Alexander Wiley, Republican Senator from Wisconsin and senior Republican on the Senate Foreign Relations Committee.

President Eisenhower was at the Augusta National Golf Club during this meeting. Tom Dewey kept in touch with him from the telephone in the bar at the King and Prince Hotel. Other kingmakers who kept in touch with the meeting and who may have been present part of the time include Nelson Rockefeller, Harold Stassen, Thomas S. Lamont, Dean Acheson, Gardner Cowles, Winthrop Aldrich and Walter Lippmann.

The participants at the St. Simon's meeting were some of the biggest names in American politics, business and the press. As described by an eye-witness observer of that meeting, "Those who came were not the heads of states, but those who give orders to heads of states,"—in other words, the kingmakers. Who was there, who got this priceless collection of prominent people together under one roof, and what they discussed and decided—should have been front-page news on every newspaper in America. These facts are interesting and important to all informed citizens. But no enterprising reporters covered this meeting of VIPs. Although three of the leading newsmen in America were present, Arthur Sulzberger of the *New York Times*, Ralph McGill of the *Atlanta Constitution*, and C. D. Jackson of *Time*, they did not print a word about this sensational meeting in their publications.

Other never-before-published details of this secret meeting make fascinating reading, even at this late date. Officially called DeBilderberg group, the U.S. kingmakers were joined on St. Simon's Island by a similarly select assortment of foreigners with whom financial and political contacts are maintained. The titular head of this secret group was Prince Bernhard of the Netherlands. The meeting was conducted with multilingual phones just like at the United Nations; one could merely push a button and get French, German or English from expert translators.

All participants arrived by corporate or private planes at the St. Simon's airport. The food was flown in from the Pierre Hotel in New York except for one seafood dinner prepared by the King and Prince Hotel. A wine list was prepared and printed especially for the meeting, with fine wines imported directly from France. The bill for the entire meeting was paid by H. J. Heinz II, President of the H. J. Heinz Company, except that David Rockefeller signed many of the bar checks. Nobody else was allowed to pay for anything.

DeBilderbergers have met once or twice a year since their first meeting at DeBilderberg Hotel in the Netherlands in May 1954. Their most recent meeting was held March 20–22, 1964, at the Rockefeller restoration at Williamsburg, Virginia.

Leading these deliberations were prominent leftwing Democrats such as Undersecretary of

State George W. Ball and former Secretary of State Dean Acheson who said after Hiss' conviction: "I will not turn my back on Alger Hiss." Like-minded foreign politicians present included Prime Minister Lester Pearson of Canada. The meetings were closed and no reports were given to the press.

The St. Simon's meeting of DeBilderbergers holds several important lessons for Americans today.

(1) It proves that there do in fact exist secret groups of persons high in finance, government and the press who meet secretly to make important plans they do not reveal to the public. DeBilderbergers is only one of these groups.

(2) It shows that these secret meetings are heavily weighted in favor of the liberal foreign viewpoint and loaded with Americans who have important financial and business contacts and investments abroad—to the exclusion of persons with a pro-American viewpoint.

(3) It shows that Republicans are in a small minority in these meetings, and are always of the liberal "me too" variety.

(4) It shows that the top level "me too" Republicans have a close social, business and political working relationship with top-level leftwing Democrats.

Highly placed New York kingmakers work toward "convergence" between the Republican and

Democratic parties so as to preserve their America Last foreign policy and eliminate foreign policy from political campaigns.

The secret kingmakers exercise their influence in both parties. In 1932 the New York kingmakers were confident that, because of the depression, whoever won the Democratic nomination, would be the next president. Their New York candidate was opposed by two presidential candidates who could not be controlled, Alfred E. Smith and Senator James Reed of Missouri. So the kingmakers made a deal with the leader of the most ruthless political machine in America, Huey Long. The New York kingmakers said that they would vote to seat Huey Long and his followers as delegates from Louisiana, although the Convention Credentials Committee had approved the anti-Long delegates. In exchange, Huey Long helped round up enough votes to nominate Franklin D. Roosevelt.

It is easy to spot the most trusted agents of the kingmakers because they are men who move with ease in and out of both parties. They appear to have a magic ability to be named to top government positions by both Republicans and Democrats. Here are a few examples:

Nelson Rockefeller, Coordinator of Latin American Affairs for the Roosevelt administration, and Republican candidate for president in 1964.

Henry Cabot Lodge, Ambassador to South Vietnam for the Kennedy and Johnson administrations, and Republican candidate for president in 1964.

Robert Strange McNamara, a man who called himself a Republican, but who served as Secretary of Defense for the Kennedy and the Johnson administrations.

C. Douglas Dillon, Undersecretary of State for the Eisenhower administration, who mysteriously was carried over as Secretary of the Treasury for the Kennedy and the Johnson administrations.

Arthur H. Dean, chief negotiator at Panmunjom for the Eisenhower administration, who carried over as disarmament adviser for the Kennedy administration.

Paul G. Hoffman, "modern Republican," who served as foreign aid head for the Truman Administration, and then was named Manager of the UN Special Fund by the Eisenhower administration.

Robert B. Anderson, who served as Secretary of the Navy and then Secretary of the Treasury under the Eisenhower administration, is now L.B.J.'s "special ambassador to work out a settlement with Panama."

For highly-placed Republicans to accept appointments from the Democrats is destructive of the two-party system. The voters expect Republicans to be Republicans, and Democrats to be Democrats.

Trading in and out of both parties confuses the issues and especially the responsibility—which is indeed the motive of the kingmakers who direct this traffic as easily as an expert playing chess.

This is also a technique which has been used by Democrats to undercut Republican opposition to Democrat policies. In 1940 during the Republican National Convention, when Roosevelt's war intervention policy was the major issue, Roosevelt boldly appointed two prominent Republicans to his cabinet: Henry L. Stimson as Secretary of War and Frank Knox as Secretary of the Navy. This was a clever move of the master politician to divide and confuse Republicans, and to prevent them from making his war policy the campaign it should have been.

Later when Roosevelt extended favors to Wendell Willkie and sent him around the world on a U.S. government bomber with an Air Force crew, this was a move designed to soften Republican opposition to Roosevelt's "grand design to appease Stalin," and it achieved considerable success.

Likewise today, President Johnson is cleverly using Republicans to cover his most controversial policies and prevent them from being issues in the 1964 campaign.

He is using Secretary of Defense Robert McNamara, a Republican, to camouflage the tragic disarmament policies of the Johnson Administration, the cancellation of such strategic weapons as the Skybolt, the RS-70, the Pluto nuclear missile, and the Nike-Zeus, and the closing down of our missile bases in Turkey and Italy.

President Johnson is using Republican C. Douglas Dillon as Secretary of the Treasury to front for the $100 billion budget, the largest peacetime budget in our history.

President Johnson is using Henry Cabot Lodge, Republican vice presidential candidate in 1960, to cover for the Administration's sellout to the Communists in South Vietnam. Vietnam should be as important and winning an issue for Republicans in 1964 as Korea was in 1952. But Republicans are handicapped from making it a campaign issue because of Henry Cabot Lodge's complicity in the tragic blunders.

Among the most influential kingmakers who profess to be Republicans is the Morgan banking group headed by Thomas S. Lamont, Jr., son of the Thomas S. Lamont who masterminded Willkie's nomination, and brother of Corliss Lamont, a leading Soviet apologist. Thomas S. Gates, the present president of Morgan Guaranty Trust Company, is the son of Thomas S. Gates, who installed Harold Stassen as president of the University of Pennsylvania in 1948.

Other New York kingmakers active in perpetuating the foreign giveaway programs which have so completely failed to stop Communism are the Averell Harriman group, which controls Brown Brothers Harriman and Company; the Rockefeller group, which controls New York's two largest banks, the Chase Manhattan Bank and the First National City Bank and which interlocks with the Morgan group through joint directors; the Whitney-Reid group which controls the *New York Herald Tribune* and its anti-Goldwater syndicated columnist Walter Lippmann; the Eugene Meyer group which controls the *Washington Post* and *Newsweek*; the Gardner Cowles group, which controls *Look Magazine*, the *Minneapolis Star*, and the *Des Moines Register*; the Henry Luce group which controls *Time*, *Life*, and *Fortune* and published the "Big Steal" attack on Senator Taft in 1952 two days ahead of *Time*'s regular issue day so as to have maximum effect on the Republican Convention Delegates.

On May 18, 1964, *Newsweek* printed pictures of some of the upper echelon kingmakers determined to stop Goldwater: General Lucius Clay of Lehman Bros., former Secretary of Defense Thomas S. Gates, president of Morgan Guaranty Trust Co., investment banker Sidney J. Weinberg, and Gardner Cowles, publisher of *Look* which provided the principal campaign piece for Rockefeller's California campaign.

The New York kingmakers' establishment includes all those financial leaders who favor a continuation of the Roosevelt-Harry Dexter White-Averell Harriman-Dean Acheson-Dean Rusk policy of *aiding* and *abetting* Red Russia and her satellites. These financiers, some of whom profess to be Republicans, have never criticized the following Democrat policies:

1) Recognizing Red Russia after three Republican Presidents refused to do so;

2) Overlooking Red Russia's violation of the Litvinov-Roosevelt agreement to permit religious freedom in Russia and to refrain from propaganda and espionage in the United States;

3) Overlooking Red Russia's failure to pay its World War I and World War II debts to us of $12,351,952,530, its post World War II debt to us of $500,000,000, and its seizure without compensation of America private property worth billions in Iron Curtain countries;

4) Condoning Red Russia's invasion of its peaceful neighbors: Finland, Latvia, Lithuania, Estonia, Poland, Czechoslovakia, Hungary, etc.;

5) Giving to Red Russia at Teheran, Yalta and Potsdam control of Eastern Europe, Manchuria, North Korea, the Kurile Islands, all World War II

anti-communist Russian refugees, plus three votes in the UN;

6) Letting China fall to the communists under the Lattimore-Acheson-Institute of Pacific Relations policies;

7) Continuing to send billions of American dollars to communists such as Tito who still proclaims, "I am a communist and nothing but a communist,"[1] and to Sukarno who told the U.S. to "go to hell with your aid";[2]

8) Accepting the continued violation of the Monroe Doctrine in Cuba;

9) Delivering U.S. wheat to Red Russia and its agents, such as the Continental Grain Company owned by French banking interests, at prices far below the cost of production and shipping.

What is the motive of the secret kingmakers?

During the Roosevelt Administration, their chief motive was surreptitiously to get the American taxpayers to protect the kingmakers' heavy investments in England and Western Europe.

Since the end of World War II, the United States foreign giveaway programs have become immensely profitable for certain Americans.

From July 1, 1946 to June 30, 1963, the U.S. gave away abroad $148,456,330,000. This is $46.7 billion *more* than the total assessed valuation of America's fifty largest cities. There are large profits to be made in acting as depositary, or fiscal agent, or issuer of letters of credit, or purchasing agent, or attorney for the foreign recipients of these immense sums, or as broker for the seller of goods purchased under the foreign aid program, both here and abroad.

The New York kingmakers, for pocketbook reasons, are extremely anxious to prevent any curtailment of the foreign giveaway program. This might come about:

1) by the election of a president who did *not* put the welfare of America secondary to the welfare of every other country from Albania to Zanzibar, or

2) by the collapse of the communist system which is the sole excuse for the foreign aid program.

Voltaire once said: "If there were no God, it would be necessary to invent Him." Time and time again, the communist regime has been saved from collapse by American diplomatic, military or economic assistance—under the America Last foreign policy dictated by the kingmakers: in 1933 when Roosevelt recognized the Soviet Union just after the food shortages and revolts caused by the liquidation of the kulaks; in 1941–42 during the Hitler-Stalin struggle; in 1953 when Stalin died; in 1956 when the Hungarian Freedom Fighters threw off the Soviet yoke in Hungary and could have touched off a wave of revolts behind the Iron

Curtain; and again in 1962–64 when Red China and the Soviet Union ran out of food.

This hidden policy of perpetuating the Red empire in order to perpetuate the high level of federal spending and control is revealed in secret studies made by the Kennedy administration.[3]

The kingmakers have a vested interest in preventing—at all cost—the election of a president such as Barry Goldwater who will let the Soviet system collapse of its own internal weaknesses, who will curtail the foreign giveaway programs, as well as the level of federal spending, and whose foreign policy will serve the best interests of the United States of America.

Also, the New York kingmakers are not opposed to the New Deal—New Frontier—Fast Deal policy of deficit financing which results in buying the people's votes with their own money. The national debt has been raised six times by the Democrats since 1961. Senator John J. Williams recently proved that Democratic administrations are responsible for $293 billion of the national debt while Republican administrations are chargeable with only $13 billion.

Since the New York kingmakers dominate the consortium which fixes the interest rate the government has to pay on its obligations, they have no incentive to see deficit financing stop. They even favor the Democrat policy of giving foreigners the right to exchange their dollars for gold or silver, but of denying this right to American citizens. The only way to stop the spend and elect policy of LBJ, supported by the kingmakers and their lackeys, is to vote for candidates *not* controlled by the kingmakers.

Part II

The Battle Continues
1968–2016

15

The Swing to the Right

1968

After Barry Goldwater's massive defeat in 1964 (61 to 39 percent), the kingmakers set out to lay a guilt trip on conservatives and hit them with the constant refrain: You conservatives had your chance; Barry Goldwater's crushing defeat proves that America will never elect a real conservative; a moderate is the best you can hope for. And Goldwater virtually abdicated his party leadership role.

The kingmakers' candidate in 1968 was New York Governor Nelson Aldrich Rockefeller. He nursed a lifelong ambition to be elected president, and 1968 was his third try. Men of impressive financial and social prestige quickly lined up behind him: Thomas S. Gates Jr., chairman of Morgan Guaranty Trust Company; Douglas Dillon, an investment banker and secretary of the Treasury in the Kennedy and Johnson administrations; Henry J. Heinz II, chairman of H. J. Heinz Company; Eugene Black, former president of the World Bank; John A. McCone, director of the Central Intelligence Agency at the time of the Cuban Missile Crisis, one of the worst U.S. intelligence failures in history; John Hay Whitney, former publisher of the interventionist-Republican *New York Herald Tribune* and one of Wendell Willkie's original supporters; and Walter N. Thayer, president of Whitney Communications Corporation. The list also included two men who had supported Lyndon B. Johnson in 1964: J. Irwin Miller, chairman of Cummins Engine Company, and Stanley Marcus, president of Neiman-Marcus.

After the filing deadline for every state primary had passed, Walter Cronkite's *CBS Evening News* reported a great "reservoir of support" for Rockefeller, and Eric Sevareid editorialized that Rockefeller's strategy was based on the assumption that many of Nixon's delegates were made of "soft glue and can become unstuck." Indeed, the Establishment had an impressive record of getting delegates "unstuck." However, Rockefeller's support among organization Republicans was very shaky, and Republican strength in his home state had declined substantially during his three terms as governor.

When Governor Ronald Reagan of California began to be discussed as the Republican presidential nominee, the pollsters moved in to preempt that possibility. In January 1968, the Harris Poll published a report headlined "Survey Shows Reagan Is Losing Strength Fast." The push-poll questions were devised to produce this verdict. Those polled were asked whether they could "agree," "disagree," or were "not sure" about such statements as: "Reagan's background as an actor is not the kind of experience needed to become President."

Reagan's political advisers theorized that Nixon and Rockefeller would deadlock, and after three to five ballots Reagan would be nominated in a brokered convention. They were wrong: in a brokered convention, the deal-making governors with their big delegations hold the trumps, not the idealists or grassroots activists.

By the time the Rockefeller and Reagan campaigns got underway, Nixon already had a big head start in the race for delegates. He had built a first-rate campaign staff and organization. He started early, worked hard, and left no stone unturned in his contacts with delegates. It was one of the best-run of all presidential campaigns. In addition, Nixon had acquired a cache of political chits by campaigning vigorously for congressional candidates in 1966. Nixon hired twenty-seven-year-old

Patrick Buchanan away from the *St. Louis Globe-Democrat* to liven up his speeches with conservative rhetoric. Nixon knew that Republicans were hungry for a conservative message, and he built a solid reputation as a good speaker who could spark Republican audiences.

The mindset of grassroots conservatives at that time could be summed up like this: a plain-talking conservative simply can't be elected president. We must back a moderate-conservative who is electable and be content with, say, 75 percent of what we want, because that is better than not winning at all. Disappointed Goldwaterites fashioned a mental image of their next presidential candidate, and Richard Nixon matched it.

On the roll call for president in Miami Beach, Nixon received 692 votes, Rockefeller 277, and Reagan 182. With Spiro Agnew as his running mate, Richard Nixon went on to defeat Hubert Humphrey in November 1968.

The surprise lesson of the 1968 presidential campaign was that a conservative could actually be elected president! Nixon campaigned as a hardline conservative, not as a moderate. His speeches were as strong as any right-winger could wish. Nixon promised fiscal responsibility, no trade with the Soviet Union, and rebuilding our nuclear superiority. His 1968 victory demolished the alleged lesson of 1964 that "a conservative can't win."

Nixon's election also proved that a president could be elected without the once-powerful Northeast and its liberal Republican officeholders. He won without New York, Pennsylvania, Massachusetts, and Michigan. Nixon owed his victory totally to conservatives. Nixon didn't owe Establishment Republicans anything. James Reston, the oracle of the *New York Times*, wrote:

> If you have any doubt about the political swing to the right in the United States, all you have to do is look around. The reaction has set in from California to New York.... It is not the politicians who are driving the people to the right, but the people who are driving even liberal politicians in that direction.[1]

Even that reliably liberal pollster Lou Harris conceded, "America is in a politically conservative mood."[2]

The "swing to the right" described by James Reston could have gone far if Richard Nixon had been a man of his word. But Nixon betrayed conservatives' hopes. Senator Hugh Scott of Pennsylvania, a prominent Rockefeller Republican, boasted to a reporter:

"We get the action and the conservatives get the rhetoric."[3]

16

Betrayal at the Top

1972

As soon as Richard Nixon moved into the White House in January 1969, he froze out the conservatives who had nominated and elected him. His capitulation to the Eastern Establishment was early and total. He gave the Rockefeller Republicans a hammerlock over all policies that mattered. In his most shocking action, Nixon appointed Henry Kissinger, Nelson Rockefeller's protégé, to be national security adviser in charge of defense and foreign policy. Nixon even named Rockefeller to the prestigious commission that enjoys wide access to U.S. intelligence information: the Foreign Intelligence Advisory Board.

On January 19, 1971, the *New York Times* published a full-page report on how policy was made in the Nixon administration. Henry Kissinger enjoyed the "authority to operate virtually as a super-Cabinet officer managing the sprawling foreign-affairs community." The *Times* quoted a secretary as joking that Kissinger's rank in the White House was "just below God." Kissinger used his extraordinary power and influence over Nixon to continue all Robert McNamara's disastrous policies of dismantling America's nuclear forces and continuing the Vietnam War on a no-win basis.

In May 1972, President Nixon went on a fateful trip to Moscow, where he signed two treaties that Kissinger had negotiated with the Soviet Union: the SALT I agreement, binding the United States to a three-to-two inferiority in nuclear missiles and submarines, and the Anti-Ballistic Missile (ABM) Treaty, giving up America's right to defend our people and cities with an anti-missile defense.[1] This ABM treaty was controversial until 2002 when, at last, President George W. Bush withdrew the United States from it.

Nixon betrayed his other 1968 campaign promises, too. He had promised to reverse "irresponsible fiscal policies," but he increased spending to enormous deficit levels, authorized more foreign giveaways, devalued the dollar twice, moved us to the then-highest interest rates in history, and on August 15, 1971, imposed price and wage controls. He persuaded Congress to reimpose an income surtax that was about to expire, even though he had campaigned against that specific tax. He fatuously announced that "I am now a Keynesian in economics."

Nixon's celebrated trip to China in February 1972 to open up trade with that communist country was widely denounced by conservatives. Barry Goldwater expressed the conservative position when he said, "As far as I'm concerned, Mr. Nixon can go to China and stay there."[2]

The liberal commentator Murray Kempton summed up the Nixon administration:

> The conservative movement lost disastrously with Barry Goldwater and survived quite healthy. It took its triumph under Mr. Nixon finally to disable it.... I am not here to advance the conservative argument, but it was at least respectable until Mr. Nixon got his hands on it.[3]

At the 1972 Republican National Convention in Miami Beach, the only real battle was fought in the convention rules committee. The Rockefeller Republicans had devised a clever plan to take back control of the Republican Party, which they had lost at the 1964 Republican National Convention. Their plan was to change the rules about the mechanics and membership of the next Republican National Convention, in 1976, in order to assure the nomination of a liberal. Mississippi state chairman Clarke Reed predicted that the liberals' proposals would assure that the 1976 nominee "would be a Javits or a Percy," referring to liberal Republican senators from New York and Illinois, respectively.

The Rockefeller plan was (1) to reapportion the convention delegates from each state according to a new formula that would divert 12 percent of the delegates to the Northeast and away from the Southern and Western states, (2) to set up a quota system for youth and minorities that would open up unlimited opportunities for delegate challenges and enable the liberals to expel legitimately elected delegates, and (3) to set up an "implementation committee" similar to the McGovern Committee, which had been a vital instrument in delivering the 1972 Democratic nomination to George McGovern.

The liberals planned their campaign for many months under the leadership of Senator Charles Percy and Representative John B. Anderson, both of Illinois. They placed their best spokesmen on the rules committee, positioned in a diamond pattern so they could work in tandem to support each other on parliamentary maneuvers. They had an impressive arsenal of emotional trigger words to buttress their position—they were working "for minorities," they were the party of the "Open Door," they urged "full participation" and "equal opportunity." They had four governors waiting outside the committee room at midnight, ready to speak if needed—Francis Sargent of Massachusetts, William Milliken of Michigan, Dan Evans of Washington, and Robert Ray of Iowa.

The conservatives had no famous names or people in high office—no senator, no cabinet official, and only one representative, James Quillen of Tennessee. The conservative fight was led by two little-known delegates, Clarke Reed of Mississippi and Tom Staggs of Louisiana.

In a dramatic rules committee vote, the conservatives won sixty-one to twenty-seven. Senator Bob Packwood muttered, "We are worse off now than we were before." The Rockefeller liberals were persistent. They took their case to the convention floor, where, after a sixty-minute debate, they lost on the roll-call vote, 434 to 910.

The rules committee battle demonstrated again that grassroots Republicans do not want to be dictated to by Eastern liberals. Republican delegates from all over the country had the patience to sit through hours of liberal harangue and vote No. The Associated Press summed up the Miami Beach convention on August 25 with reluctant admiration for conservatives:

> The Party that met here this week ended
> its sessions with the Ronald Reagans and
> Barry Goldwaters and John Towers in
> firm control of its direction, rather than
> the Nelson Rockefellers and Charles
> Percys.

Delegates closed ranks and backed the incumbent Nixon for renomination because "We must not be divisive" and "At least he's better than a Democrat." Or so Republicans thought until it was too late to make a different choice.

To make his 1972 convention nominating speech, Nixon selected Nelson Rockefeller, then in his fourth term as governor of New York. Richard Nixon and Spiro Agnew were renominated for president and vice president and then reelected in November 1972. They were helped by the Democrats' error in nominating George McGovern with his "new politics" of "acid, amnesty, and abortion." Nixon-Agnew enjoyed a landslide victory; the Electoral College count was 520 to 17.

The Accidental President

1974

The Eastern Establishment and the kingmakers were probably well satisfied with the way Republican President Nixon allowed Henry Kissinger to continue the foreign and defense policies of Democratic Presidents Kennedy and Johnson. But Nelson Rockefeller wasn't satisfied with directing policy through his surrogate, Henry Kissinger, because he still cherished his lifelong ambition to become president. His dreams having been thrice dashed—in 1960, 1964, and 1968—Rockefeller realized that no Republican National Convention would ever nominate him. So he planned an alternative route to the White House that would bypass the convention—an amendment to the Constitution providing for the president to nominate a new vice president in the event of a vacancy in the office.

It's not easy to amend the U.S. Constitution. To accomplish this task, Rockefeller called on Herbert Brownell, one of the cleverest lawyers of the New York establishment. Brownell had managed Tom Dewey's campaign in 1948, engineered the smear-campaign against Taft in 1952, and been a chief adviser to the liberal New York City mayor John Lindsay. Brownell wrote the proposed Twenty-fifth Amendment, marshaled the talking points, lobbied it through Congress, and then lobbied it through three-fourths of the state legislatures to ratification in 1967—all without any publicity. He made it appear so reasonable, so necessary, so noncontroversial.

The Twenty-fifth Amendment is one of our longest constitutional amendments, and few people read it before or after it was passed. Under cover of its wordiness, its real purpose was to give us a president who was *appointed* to the position—but never nominated by a national convention or elected by the American people.

To make the Twenty-fifth Amendment work for Rockefeller, Vice President Spiro Agnew had to be removed first. Agnew was accused of failing to report $29,500 on his income tax return and was offered a plea bargain he couldn't refuse. By pleading *nolo contendere,* he escaped a felony conviction and jail sentence. The price, of course, was vacating the office. Agnew resigned as vice president on October 10,

1973. President Nixon then used the new Twenty-fifth Amendment to appoint Representative Gerald Ford as vice president. Congressional confirmation was no problem because Ford was a popular member.

Ford had already proved he was a man whom the Establishment could count on to take orders.[1] He had been a member of the Warren Commission assigned to investigate the assassination of President John F. Kennedy. Then came the Watergate scandal causing Nixon to resign in disgrace on August 8, 1974. Nixon's resignation bumped Gerald Ford into the Oval Office. That's how Ford became the one and only U.S. president who was never elected by the American people. When Ford entered the White House, Henry Kissinger was waiting to advise him how to use the Twenty-fifth Amendment. Eleven days after Ford became president, he appointed Nelson Rockefeller as vice president.

The Twenty-fifth Amendment made all this happen. For the next two years, Rockefeller served as vice president, just a heartbeat away from his lifelong goal. In a CBS television documentary on this appointment, Walter Cronkite commented that "the Rockefellers are the epitome of America's permanent establishment."

The Establishment repeatedly reveals its irritation with the U.S. Constitution and the desire to change it so that the powers that be can more easily control the selection of our president and other powerful officials. Every few years a new group of self-important politicians, who think they are smarter than the Founding Fathers, meet in secret to plot changes in the Constitution in order to control the choice of U.S. presidents.

A bunch of powerful movers and shakers met to explore these goals in the Mayflower Hotel in Washington, D.C., on December 5, 1986. The participants agreed on a plan to make major changes in the Constitution, asserting that the Constitution needed to be updated because it was impeding solutions to current problems. This was no rag-tag bunch of impatient politicians or utopian-minded professors. The group consisted of some of the most influential and important men in America.

A spirit of quiet arrogance pervaded the Mayflower discussions. Clearly, this little group saw itself as possessing vision and talent comparable to that of James Madison, George Washington, Benjamin Franklin, and the other Founding Fathers who met in Independence Hall in Philadelphia in 1787. This Mayflower group, calling itself the Committee on the Constitutional System (CCS), planned to make Americans dissatisfied with our Constitution and willing to accept structural changes. The CCS hoped that this publicity would escalate into a demand to call a new constitutional convention to rewrite the U.S. Constitution.

CCS's chairman and driving force was Lloyd N. Cutler, a prominent Washington lawyer and adviser to Presidents Jimmy Carter and Bill Clinton. Other influential members listed in CCS materials, several of whom were present at the Mayflower meeting, included former the secretary of the Treasury C. Douglas Dillon, the former secretary of defense and World Bank president Robert S. McNamara, the former chairman of the Senate Foreign Relations Committee J. William Fulbright, and a favorite Establishment historian, James MacGregor Burns. The meeting was bipartisan. It included Republicans—Governor Richard Thornburgh of Pennsylvania, who later became President George H. W. Bush's attorney general, and Senator Charles Mathias Jr. of Maryland.

The CCS had been toying with radical ideas for rewriting the U.S. Constitution for some years prior to the Mayflower meeting. In 1985, CCS published a 334-page book called *Reforming American Government*, a collection of forty papers critiquing the Constitution. The papers explored different approaches, but the persistent message was dissatisfaction with our Constitution. The papers were peppered with words of distress such as "problem," "crisis," "reform," "defects," "decay," and "risk." The *raison d'être* of the CCS volume was neatly summarized in the lead quotation from Robert S. McNamara on the back cover:

It is tempting to believe that our constitutional system, having survived for
almost 200 years, can handle the daunt-
ing challenges it now confronts. But
common sense warns us that it may not
be so. These "papers" are reassuring evidence that the creativity and sagacity of
the original framers are still alive in this
country.

The Mayflower speakers referred to themselves
as "the parliamentary government group." The clear
aim of the group was to change the structure of
the U.S. government by replacing our separation
of powers with a European parliamentary system.
CCS members believed they could improve on
James Madison's assumption that the "preservation
of liberty requires that the three great departments
of power should be separate and distinct."

The CCS approved a report asserting that our
separation of powers has produced chronic "con-
frontation, indecision and deadlock." CCS materials
outlined more than a dozen specific plans to change
America into a parliamentary system, such as giving
the president the power to dissolve Congress and
call new elections, eliminating the Senate's treaty-
ratification power, eliminating the Twenty-second
Amendment, which limits presidents to two terms,

and forcing the taxpayers to finance congressional election campaigns.

This secret Mayflower meeting on December 5, 1986, was reported exclusively by me.[2] A month later, on January 11, 1987, the *New York Times* discovered it.

18

Climbing up the Hill

1976

By 1975, conservatives were taking inventory of Gerald Ford's record as our first unelected president. In matters where he acted on his own, his record was good. He resisted intense pressure to impose gasoline rationing or price and wage controls. He was not stampeded into bailing out New York City with federal funds.

In matters where he followed the advice of his two chief appointees, Vice President Nelson Rockefeller and Secretary of State Henry Kissinger, however, Ford gave us a steady succession of deficits at home and defeats abroad. Heavy spending fueled galloping inflation, giving us the then-largest peacetime deficit in history.

Ford kept Henry Kissinger in control of our foreign policy, military policy, and intelligence. Kissinger was the architect of the Paris Peace Accords of 1973, which ended the Vietnam War on substantially the same humiliating terms on which it could have been ended four years earlier when Nixon first appointed Kissinger in 1969. Kissinger also started negotiations for a new treaty with Panama to surrender our U.S. canal. He was a forceful advocate of this giveaway of one of America's greatest military and commercial assets.

From the very hour he took office as president in August 1974, Ford's statements were filled with sycophantic praise of Kissinger. Representative Edward Derwinski (R-Ill.) remarked, "The President is a captive of Henry K. The subordinate is controlling his chief."[1]

Meanwhile, First Lady Betty Ford was making blunt overtures to the emerging feminist movement. In August 1975, she appeared on CBS's *60 Minutes* and announced her support of legalized abortion and the Equal Rights Amendment. She suggested that premarital sex might cut down on the divorce rate and said she would not criticize her daughter if she were to enter into a non-marital affair.

The 1976 Republican National Convention in Kansas City promised to be the most exciting convention since 1952. Conservatives were starting to flex their muscles again, and a serious movement for Ronald Reagan was gathering steam. The liberals and moderates, of course, supported Gerald Ford, who had proved he would take orders from the kingmakers. The Establishment was aided by the cult of incumbency: Republican incumbents close ranks to protect each other.

To outmaneuver the occupant of the White House and win the nomination, Reagan needed a winning strategy, but his 1976 campaign manager, John Sears, was inadequate for the task. He tried to run Reagan as a moderate with charisma. That didn't work; Ford won the New Hampshire primary by 1,317 votes.

Reagan's campaign picked up momentum only after local conservatives took the campaign into their own hands, made effective use of volunteers, and encouraged Reagan to take a strong stand on issues such as the Panama Canal giveaway, Henry Kissinger, détente, and the Human Life Amendment. Reagan then scored brilliant victories in North Carolina under the leadership of Senator Jesse Helms and in Texas with the leadership of J. Evetts and Rosalind Haley.

Reagan's speeches in the primaries identified the major issues, especially the overriding issue of the survival of America in the face of the gigantic Soviet missile threat. He correctly identified Kissinger's worldview and explained that Kissinger's policy was to surrender U.S. strategic superiority to the

Soviet Union, missile by missile, bomber by bomber, submarine by submarine. Reagan bought a half-hour of television time on March 31, 1976, raising what the media labeled "the Kissinger issue," and quoted Kissinger as telling Admiral Elmo Zumwalt, "The day of the United States is past and today is the day of the Soviet Union. My job as Secretary of State is to negotiate the most acceptable second-best position available."

Two weeks before Kansas City, the press reported that Ford and Reagan were neck and neck with 124 delegates uncommitted, sufficient to swing it either way. That made it one of the closest conventions of the twentieth century.

The decisive factor of the 1976 Convention was the platform. A first-term senator from a southern state, Jesse Helms, decided that the 1976 Republican platform was the place to stand and fight for the conservative principles that had eroded under Nixon, Ford, and Kissinger. Helms wanted to get the convention to adopt a strong Republican platform that really stood for principles we could be proud of, instead of the appeasement and retreat that characterized the Nixon and Ford administrations. Helms led the battle to adopt a platform based on what he called "morality in foreign policy." This plank criticized the giveaway of the Panama Canal, détente with the Soviet Union, and unilateral concessions on nuclear testing. The Helms platform directly attacked the foreign and national defense policies of incumbent Republican President Gerald Ford and Henry Kissinger.

It was a tremendous victory when the convention adopted Jesse Helms's platform, which completely repudiated the Nixon-Ford-Kissinger foreign policy. The Republican Party turned away from accommodation of communist Russia and toward victory over the evil empire. It set the stage for Reagan's determination that our attitude toward the Soviet Union should be "we win and they lose." The platform showed the country that the majority of Republicans stood solidly in favor of repudiating the RINOs (Republicans In Name Only) and rebuilding the party based on conservative principles.

The 1976 platform was not just about foreign policy; 1976 was the first Republican National Convention when the emerging pro-family movement raised its voice in politics. Republicans dared to challenge the U.S. Supreme Court in this first Republican National Convention after *Roe v. Wade*. The platform subcommittee voted thirteen to one to include a plank to "protest the Supreme Court's intrusion into the family structure" and pledged to "seek enactment of a constitutional amendment to restore protection of the right to life for unborn children." The plank was easily approved by the full Convention.

When it became obvious that the convention delegates were overwhelmingly in favor of the Reagan foreign policy and that Ford was heading toward a humiliating defeat on a roll call, the Ford forces moved to adopt the Helms platform unanimously on a voice vote.

The 1976 Convention in Kansas City nominated Gerald Ford by a narrow vote of 1,187 to 1,070. A switch of only fifty-nine votes would have nominated Reagan. When Ronald and Nancy Reagan came into the hall on the final night, the demonstration was thunderous. NBC's David Brinkley commented, "Gerald Ford has the votes, but Reagan has the enthusiasm."

At the very end of the session, Ford spontaneously turned the microphone over to Reagan, who delivered one of the most dramatic speeches in the history of political conventions. Speaking extemporaneously for less than five minutes, Reagan reminded his delegates of their accomplishment: "Our platform is a banner of bold, unmistakable colors with no pastel shades." That needed to be made clear because the Ford forces had avoided a roll-call vote that would have demonstrated to the television audience the convention's repudiation of the Kissinger policies.

In the debates between Gerald Ford and Jimmy Carter in the fall, however, Republicans again had to endure a candidate who failed to come to grips with the major issues of the day: how to reverse the Kissinger policies of making America second-best to the Soviet Union and how to reduce federal spending in order to cut taxes and the inflation-causing deficit. Ford committed the biggest blunder in presidential debate history when he denied that the Soviet Union controlled the countries behind the Iron Curtain.

The kingmakers shed no tears when the ticket of Gerald Ford and Robert Dole was defeated by Jimmy Carter in November 1976. They had already sized up Carter as a man who would make no significant change in foreign or defense policies.

The nomination of Jimmy Carter by the 1976 Democratic National Convention is another example of Establishment tentacles extending into both political parties. More than 60 percent of Democrats who voted in the 1976 primaries voted for a candidate other than Jimmy Carter. Nevertheless, the national media, including the *New York Times* and *Time,* proclaimed Carter the invincible candidate for the Democratic nomination.

Zbigniew Brzezinski, President Carter's National Security Adviser, was another protégé of Rockefeller and practically a mirror image of Henry Kissinger. In his book *Between Two Ages*, Brzezinski was blunt in declaring that "the nation-state is gradually yielding its sovereignty" and "the fiction of sovereignty...is clearly no longer compatible with reality."[2] He even called for "a national constitutional convention to re-examine the nation's formal institutional framework" in order to consider "the desirability of imitating the various European regionalization reforms."[3]

Gerald Rafshoon, one of Carter's media advisers, later said, "One of the most fortunate accidents in the early campaign and critical to his building support where it counted was Jimmy Carter's membership in the Trilateral Commission." The Trilateral Commission, a power clique of some two hundred banking, commercial, political, and communications leaders, was the brainchild of David Rockefeller and Brzezinski. They had the foresight in 1973 to extend membership in this wealthy and prestigious group to a little-known one-term Georgia governor named Jimmy Carter.

When Carter entered the White House, Trilateral members flooded into the new administration's cabinet and sub-cabinet positions, including Vice President Walter Mondale, National Security Adviser Zbigniew Brzezinski, Secretary of State Cyrus Vance, Secretary of Defense Harold Brown, Secretary of the Treasury Michael Blumenthal, Ambassador to the United Nations Andrew Young, Deputy Secretary of State Warren Christopher, Assistant Secretary of State for East Asian and Pacific Affairs Richard Holbrooke, Under Secretary of State for Policy Planning W. Anthony Lake, Panama Canal Treaty negotiator Sol Linowitz, Ambassador at Large for Nuclear Power Negotiations Gerald Smith, Delegate to the Law of the Sea Conference Elliot Richardson, and Arms Control and Disarmament Agency Director Paul Warnke.

The chief legacy of the Carter administration was the ratification in 1978 of two treaties to give away the U.S.-built canal at Panama—one of the greatest man-made achievements in world history—to the drug-smuggling communist dictator Omar Torrijos. *Cui bono*? The chief lobbyists for this giveaway of U.S. property were the New York banks, which had outstanding claims against Panama of almost three billion dollars.

It didn't take Barry Goldwater long to declare that those who nominated Jimmy Carter and staffed his administration were essentially the same crowd who had controlled Republican presidential nominations for so many years and that they had the same goals. In his 1979 book, *With No Apologies*, Goldwater wrote that the goal of these unelected rulers is "the creation of a worldwide economic power superior to the political governments of the nation-states involved. They believe the abundant materialism they propose to create will overwhelm existing differences. As managers and creators of the system, they will rule the future."[4]

Explaining the relationship between the financial powers and politics, Goldwater said that David Rockefeller's Trilateral Commission "is intended to be the vehicle for multinational consolidation of the commercial and banking interests by seizing control of the political government of the United States."

Goldwater quoted from the Trilateral Commission's May 30, 1975, report calling for "centralized economic and social planning" and a "program to lower the job expectations of those who receive a college education."[5] Goldwater was one of the earliest to recognize the multinationals' long-range scheme to induce Americans to accept a dumbed-down school system and a lower standard of living in order to compete in the global economy with cheap Third World labor.

19

Victory for Conservatives

1980

As the 1980 Republican National Convention approached, conservatives were fairly well united behind Ronald Reagan. This was his third try for the presidency, he was comfortable with his conservative beliefs, and his followers had swelled in numbers and commitment.

The Eastern Establishment candidate was George H. W. Bush. When he defeated Reagan in the Iowa caucuses 31 percent to 29 percent, Bush appeared to have the momentum ("Big Mo," as he giddily called it), and the kingmakers were encouraged to believe they could exercise their customary control over the nominating process.

Then came the dramatic debate in New Hampshire. Under the sponsorship of the local newspaper, the debate was to be limited to the frontrunners

Bush and Reagan, excluding the other candidates—John Anderson, Howard Baker, Bob Dole, and Philip Crane. When the Federal Election Commission ruled that the event would be an illegal campaign contribution by the newspaper to the two principal candidates, Reagan volunteered to cover the expenses of the debate after Bush refused to split the $3,500 tab.

The four other candidates showed up anyway, with Bush still refusing to admit them to the debate. When Reagan tried to explain the situation to the live radio audience, the moderator ordered Reagan's microphone cut off. The ordinarily genial Reagan, showing leadership under stress, responded, "I am paying for this microphone, Mr. Green!" and invited the other candidates to join the debate. Reagan then swamped Bush in the New Hampshire primary and the horse race was on.

The next test was the big Illinois primary on March 18, and the polls were pointing to a victory for Representative John Anderson of Rockford. Originally elected as a conservative, Anderson had caught Potomac fever and steadily moved left, becoming a favorite of the media.[1] The tide turned in the final week before the primary after Stop ERA activists, then a major political force in Illinois, put forth an all-out effort for Ronald Reagan. Reagan carried Illinois 48 percent to 37 percent, and it became clear who really had the "Big Mo" in the 1980 race.

When GOP delegates gathered in Detroit for their convention that July, Reagan's nomination was assured, and the real question was who would be his running mate. Conservatives unfortunately were badly divided among Congressman Jack Kemp, Senator Paul Laxalt, and Senator Jesse Helms. The Establishment, of course, wanted George Bush.

Realizing they couldn't stop Ronald Reagan's nomination, the liberal Republicans developed an extraordinary game plan, one of the most unusual grabs for power in the history of the American presidency. On Wednesday, July 16, the third evening of the convention, while delegates at Joe Louis Arena were plodding through the roll call that produced 1,939 votes for Reagan, thirty-seven for John Anderson, and thirteen for George Bush, Henry Kissinger was on the sixty-ninth floor of the Renaissance Plaza Hotel, a few blocks away, promoting an incredible deal under which he, not Reagan, would exercise the powers of the presidency. If he had succeeded, it would have been a complete restructuring of the executive branch of the government.

The cover for this proposed transfer of power from a constitutionally elected president into the hands of an unelected man who was not even eligible for the office (because he was not a "natural born citizen") was to be a Ronald Reagan–Gerald Ford "dream ticket." That's how the idea was floated, but the details were not revealed. The reason the Establishment insisted on Gerald Ford as vice president was that he could be counted on to take orders from Henry Kissinger.

Speaking as the negotiator for Ford, Kissinger demanded that Reagan agree to turn over to Ford as vice president supervisory authority over the National Security Council, which controls U.S. foreign and military policies, the Office of Management and Budget, which controls federal budgeting and the purposes for which our tax dollars are spent, and the Council of Economic Advisers, which directs U.S. economic policies.

This deal was announced as a "co-presidency," but in fact so little power would remain in Reagan's hands that he would be president in name only. When CBS's Dan Rather stuck a microphone in my face on the convention floor and asked my opinion, I said, "It's completely unconstitutional. It's a plan to give Gerald Ford control of foreign policy, defense policy, and the budget, and that would leave President Reagan with little more than the Bureau of Indian Affairs."

Reagan's aides described themselves as "astonished" at the scope of the power that Kissinger demanded on behalf of Ford. The team of Rowland

Evans and Robert Novak reported that Ford's price for going on the ticket with Reagan was the appointment of Henry Kissinger as secretary of state. Reagan had stated publicly that he would not appoint Kissinger, so the ambitious Kissinger worked the co-presidency deal through his old friend, Gerald Ford. The *New York Daily News* reported that Ford nurtured such animosity against Reagan that in March 1980 Ford told friends, "Before this is over, I will get my pound of flesh out of that guy."

Back at Joe Louis Arena on that fateful Wednesday evening, Gerald and Betty Ford visited two network skyboxes high above the convention floor and promoted the Reagan-Ford "dream ticket," and Walter Cronkite broke the news of the "co-presidency" deal. It became obvious that the networks were part of Ford's bargaining apparatus, and the media eagerly supported the plot.

The pressure on Ronald Reagan from powerful people to accept the Ford-Kissinger deal became overwhelming, and there was no countervailing pressure from a united conservative movement for any alternative vice presidential candidate. Most Reagan delegates didn't know what was happening behind closed doors. Believing he might not be able to hold out if the Ford negotiators hammered him all night, Reagan telephoned George Bush at 11:37 on Wednesday night and told him to come to the convention rostrum immediately. Already in his pajamas, Bush was the most surprised man in Detroit.

Appearing before the delegates, Reagan made his midnight announcement that he had chosen George Bush to be his running mate, praising Bush as "a man who told me he can enthusiastically support the Platform across the board."

That night, Reagan saved America from its closest brush with a bloodless palace coup. If the plot had succeeded and Republicans regained the White House, Henry Kissinger would have become our de facto ruler. When I had met with Reagan in his office in Los Angeles on March 28, 1980, before the convention, the one thing I asked him was never to appoint Henry Kissinger to any important post. Reagan promised me, and he kept that promise.

With hindsight, it is easy to see that Reagan would have won in 1980 no matter who was his running mate, but no one knew that on July 16 in Detroit. Conservatives swallowed hard and accepted Reagan's choice of George H. W. Bush.

The Republican platform adopted on Tuesday evening in Detroit, like the platform adopted in Kansas City in 1976, repudiated the Kissinger policies toward the Soviet Union. The 1980 platform pledged a strategy "to achieve overall military and technological *superiority* over the Soviet Union;

[and] to accept no arms control agreement…which locks the United States into a position of military inferiority."

Meanwhile, trying to create political mischief, the media focused on the Equal Rights Amendment (ERA) as the convention's hottest issue. The effort to remove the pro-ERA plank four years earlier in Kansas City had failed narrowly, so a close vote was expected. The radical feminists had no problem getting plenty of favorable media coverage with Helen Milliken, wife of the governor of Michigan; Margaret Heckler, a U.S. representative from Massachusetts and member of the platform committee; and Mary Dent Crisp, the Republican Party co-chairman. They all predicted that ERA would remain part of the platform.

ERA had been in the Republican platform since 1940, and the Stop ERAers were determined to remove it from the 1980 platform. The media were shocked when the human resources subcommittee, chaired by Representative Trent Lott of Mississippi, voted eleven to four for a Women's Rights section that excluded ERA, and the media went into cardiac arrest when the full platform committee approved the subcommittee's action by a vote of ninety to nine.[2]

The 1980 Republican platform again affirmed "support of a constitutional amendment to restore protection of the right to life for unborn children. We also support the Congressional efforts to restrict the use of taxpayers' dollars for abortion." The feminists' effort to weaken the pro-life plank supporting a human life amendment failed in the platform committee seventy-five to eighteen.

After ERA was expunged, Mary Dent Crisp shed real tears before the television cameras—and then left the Republican Party to support John Anderson, who did his best as an independent candidate to defeat Ronald Reagan, getting 7 percent of the popular vote.

The media, the pollsters, and the feminists all predicted that on Election Day angry voters would punish those opposed to ERA. The results were the opposite. November 4, 1980, was a bad day for the feminists, starting with the election of President Ronald Reagan. In 1978, Congress had passed an unprecedented extension of the deadline for ratification of the ERA. In 1980, the sponsors of that extension—Birch Bayh of Indiana in the Senate and Elizabeth Holtzman of New York in the House, went down to defeat. Of the three women who ran for the U.S Senate, the anti-ERA Paula Hawkins of Florida was elected while pro-ERA feminists Elizabeth Holtzman and Colorado's Mary Buchanan were defeated. The original sponsor of comprehensive federal daycare for all children, another major goal of the feminist movement, Representative John Brademas of Indiana, was defeated. The Stop ERA movement won an unpredicted victory in Iowa on November 4, when a proposed state version of the ERA was rejected in a referendum 55 percent to 45 percent.

Ronald Reagan's election profoundly changed politics in America. Reagan ended the Nixon-Kissinger era of détente and surrender. Reagan mainstreamed conservatism based on middle-American fiscal and family values. Reagan's vision of conservatism consisted of four specific elements: limited government with lower taxes, personal responsibility that rejects taxpayer handouts, military superiority to protect American independence and to defeat Soviet communism, and respect for life and family values. Each of these four elements has a large constituency and attracted many conservative and pro-family Democrats and independents to vote Republican. Reagan gave Americans a choice, *not* an echo of all the previous presidential campaigns. He announced his change of direction in his First Inaugural Address: "In this present crisis, government is not the solution to our problem; government *is* the problem."

20

Defining Conservatism in Dallas

1984

Ronald Reagan and George Bush were easily renominated in 1984 in one of the most harmonious of all Republican National Conventions. That convention adopted a Republican platform that enunciated Reagan-style conservative and pro-family goals at home and abroad. A strengthened pro-life plank was adopted that has remained substantially unchanged through the conventions of 1988, 1992, 1996, 2000, 2004, 2008, and 2012:

> The unborn child has a fundamental individual right to life which cannot be infringed. We therefore reaffirm our support for a human life amendment to the Constitution, and we endorse

legislation to make clear that the Four-
teenth Amendment's protections apply
to unborn children. We oppose the use
of public revenues for abortion and
will eliminate funding for organizations which advocate or support abortion…. We reaffirm our support for the
appointment of judges at all levels of the
judiciary who respect traditional family values and the sanctity of innocent
human life.

Senator Trent Lott chaired the platform committee. The pro-life plank wasn't particularly controversial except for a couple of tantrums staged for
the media by Senator Lowell Weicker and Representative Nancy Johnson, both from Connecticut.
A lone feminist delegate's attempt to reinsert the
Equal Rights Amendment in the platform lacked
any support. The full convention adopted the platform on a voice vote.

Ronald Reagan won reelection in November
1984 because the Republican nominee and the platform offered voters a clear-cut choice on the issues
that mattered to Americans—national defense,
foreign policy, communism, fiscal policy, and social
and family policies. Voters didn't have any difficulty

telling the difference between Reagan and Walter Mondale.

The 1984 platform didn't duck controversial issues. It took a strong stand on taxes, the protection of human life, the Equal Rights Amendment, parents' rights in public schools, gay rights, quotas, child care, education, the judiciary, pornography, guns, welfare, the United Nations and UNESCO, and an anti-missile defense. Reagan's courageous and dramatic tax cut started an unprecedented economic boom. Instead of Kissinger-style pessimism, Reagan offered a vision of morning in America:

> Don't give up your ideals, don't compromise. Don't turn to expedience…. We can have that shining city on the hill—but we can have it only through God's grace, our own courage, and our own will to abide by the faith of our fathers…. Let us all go from this place, this night, and set our sights on that shining city on a hill.

The result was that Ronald Reagan decisively defeated the ticket of Walter Mondale and Geraldine Ferraro. The pro-family movement had doubled the conservative vote. The twenty-seven million conservatives who had voted for Barry

Goldwater in 1964 grew to fifty-four million in 1984.

Ronald Reagan's greatest achievement was to provoke the stunning collapse of the Soviet empire. As Margaret Thatcher summed it up, "Ronald Reagan won the Cold War without firing a shot." Victory over communism happened because Reagan demanded it, both in rhetoric and in policy decisions. In 1981, he proclaimed at the University of Notre Dame, "The West won't contain Communism. It will transcend Communism." In 1983 he dared to label the Soviet Union an "evil empire." On June 12, 1987, on a trip to the Brandenburg Gate in Berlin, he flung down the gauntlet: "Mr. Gorbachev, tear down this Wall!"

Reagan believed that we didn't have to accept a future built on Khrushchev's "peaceful coexistence," George Kennan's "containment," Richard Nixon's détente, Gorbachev's perestroika, or Henry Kissinger's treaties that accepted U.S. strategic inferiority to the Soviet Union. In a television address on March 23, 1983, he called on America to build an anti-missile defense—the Strategic Defense Initiative—to protect the American people against the giant ICBMs in which the Soviets had so much of their economy invested. The media ridiculed the proposal as "Star Wars."

Reagan's Cold War victory was nailed down on October 12, 1986, at Reykjavík, Iceland.[1] Gorbachev offered to cut his offensive nuclear weapons to zero if only Reagan would abandon plans to build an anti-missile defense. Reagan was hammered unmercifully by the Soviets and the media, and even by his own State Department, but he never backed down from his position that America must never relinquish our right to build an anti-missile defense. As he departed from the last negotiation, cameras caught him slumping into the back seat of his limousine, alone, without support or encouragement from anyone.

The media reported that Reykjavík was a failure and that the failure was Reagan's fault. *Time*'s cover screamed "Sunk by Star Wars." But Reykjavík was where Reagan won it. His personal courage and foresight in rejecting Gorbachev's proposal deprived the Soviet leader of the means to remain competitive with the United States in the arms race. That was the beginning of the end of the Evil Empire.

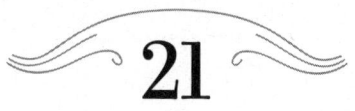

21

Bidin' My Time

1988

When the 1988 presidential primaries began, all the Republican hopefuls proclaimed they would carry forward the conservative agenda. None proclaimed himself a liberal or even a moderate. The power center of the Republican Party had moved right, south, and west. None of the extreme loyalties and bitter animosities that had deeply divided the Republican Party in previous pre-convention posturing was evident in 1988.

Nevertheless, a spirited contest took place to choose Reagan's successor. Some conservatives believed that Representative Jack Kemp of New York was the ideological successor to Reagan because he was the author of the Kemp-Roth tax cut and an eloquent advocate of Reagan's SDI. But the conservative movement did not unite behind

Kemp. Also in the running was Bob Dole, and a well-organized campaign was launched for Pat Robertson.

Establishment kingmakers united behind George Herbert Walker Bush. For the eight years of the Reagan administration, he had played his role of vice president flawlessly, as though he were singing George Gershwin's "Bidin' My Time." Easily winning the presidential nomination, Bush made no objection to the re-adoption of a Reaganesque platform at the national convention in New Orleans. The family and community subcommittee, by a vote of eleven to three, adopted the same pro-life plank that was in the 1984 platform. With Nebraska Governor Kay Orr as chairman of the full platform committee, the convention approved the platform by a unanimous voice vote.

The feminists' one major effort at New Orleans was on behalf of federally controlled and federally financed daycare as a new middle-class entitlement, reflecting their belief that it is oppressive to expect mothers to take care of their own children. The pro-family counterattack was to advocate a child tax credit in the income tax code so that parents can spend their own money for the child care of their choice. That proved to be the winning argument.

Senator Gordon Humphrey of New Hampshire led rallies to demand that Bush choose a conservative running mate. Bush responded by selecting the conservative Senator Dan Quayle of Indiana, who had endeared himself to the pro-family movement by defeating Birch Bayh, the chief sponsor of the Equal Rights Amendment.

In November 1988, the Reagan coalition, including both fiscal and social conservatives, loyally stuck together for George Bush, assuming that he would continue Reagan's agenda. Indeed, voters almost looked upon Bush's election in 1988 as voting for Ronald Reagan's "third term."

Bush had the good fortune to draw Michael Dukakis, the governor of Massachusetts, as his Democratic opponent. While most Democrats were running away from the "L-word" or muffling their liberalism, Dukakis proclaimed himself "a liberal Democrat" and "a card-carrying member" of the American Civil Liberties Union. He didn't seem to realize that what plays well in the Kennedy environs simply doesn't play in Peoria.

Dukakis was soft on criminals at the expense of law-abiding citizens and victims. He was the leading advocate of Massachusetts' unique system of giving unsupervised weekend passes to convicted murderers who had been sentenced to life without parole, a policy personified by Willie Horton.[1] Dukakis vetoed a bill to require public school teachers to lead pupils in the Pledge of Allegiance every morning. Dukakis was vociferously pro-abortion and pro-abortion-funding, and he endorsed gay rights laws.

Dukakis gave us liberalism in one package. He was a synthesis of Walter Mondale on taxes, Ted Kennedy and Tip O'Neill on spending, Geraldine Ferraro on abortion, and George McGovern on foreign policy. Since Dukakis, no politician wants to be called a liberal any more.

Bush campaigned enthusiastically on the social issues. Media-manager Michael Deaver and speechwriter Peggy Noonan made Bush look and sound like Reagan. The media's attacks on Bush for exploiting social issues elevated his standing with the voters. In a shocked voice, Dan Rather reported on the *CBS Evening News* that his network's own polls showed that the majority of Americans favor schoolchildren reciting the Pledge of Allegiance "even if it's unconstitutional" (which it is not).

In 1988, George Bush's campaign verbally offered the voters "a choice not, an echo" on patriotic, social, and pro-life issues—plus the fiscal promise that he dramatically made in his acceptance speech in New Orleans: "Read my lips. No new taxes!" The voters found it easy to make Bush a big winner.

22

The Man Who Didn't Learn

1992

As soon as George Bush became president in January 1989, he reverted to the big-government and globalist policies sought by his old 1980 campaign patrons instead of following the policies of the man to whom he owed his presidency, Ronald Reagan. High taxes, big domestic federal spending, foreign handouts, taxpayer-subsidized foreign trade, and a globalist foreign policy became the hallmarks of the Bush administration. It was as though Bush hadn't learned anything from his years as Reagan's understudy.

Almost the only conservative thing Bush did in the four years of his presidency was to appoint Clarence Thomas to the Supreme Court. The key to receiving any political or social goodies from the Bush White House was to be identified as a pre-Iowa-in-1980 "Bushie."

Bush was a willing tool for a foreign interventionist agenda. Henry Kissinger, author of the disastrous SALT I agreements with the Soviet Union and the humiliating Paris Peace Accords with North Vietnam, had been barred from policymaking about Russia during the eight Reagan years. President Bush appointed one of Kissinger's top two associates, Brent Scowcroft, as his national security adviser and the other, Lawrence Eagleburger, to run the State Department.

The guidance of the Kissinger group was evident in such foreign policy judgments as siding with Mikhail Gorbachev instead of Boris Yeltsin during the Russian transition from communism, the resuscitation of the then-discredited United Nations, and Bush's petty refusal to credit Ronald Reagan with winning the Cold War.

President Bush's global orientation became apparent in his address to Congress on September 11, 1990, just after returning from a meeting with Soviet President Gorbachev. The old Soviet Union was breaking up, and Bush proclaimed that his objective was "a new world order." The first time he used the phrase it may have been just a bit of exotic rhetoric that sounded scholarly. But Bush became enamored of it and began to use it in important speeches, including his State of the Union Address on January 29, 1991. Fred Barnes said that the phrase "new world order" became all but holy writ, and White House speechwriters routinely included it in every military or foreign policy speech by the president. Bush never defined what he meant by "new world order"—he left that task to his successor, Bill Clinton.

After leaving the White House, Bush made no secret of his alignment with the internationalists and the multinational corporations. Like Henry Kissinger, Bush became a spokesman for subsidized trade with corrupt Asian regimes, making at least fifteen trips to China.

George Bush's biggest political mistake was to put through the largest single tax increase ever imposed up to that time, thereby reneging on his ringing "read my lips" declaration of 1988. Bush stubbornly refused to fire his unpopular economic adviser, Richard Darman, who had given the bad advice about raising taxes. Darman told conservatives, "Nobody believed that promise anyway." But they had believed Bush, and that's why his betrayal was so damaging.

Pat Buchanan articulated the conservative message and received a big vote for president in the New Hampshire primary, but the renomination of President Bush at the 1992 Republican National

Convention in Houston was a foregone conclusion. After all, Bush was the incumbent—and Republicans are supposed to stick with incumbents.

Bush made no overtures to the Reagan Democrats who had swelled Ronald Reagan's margin of victory in 1980 and 1984, voters who were motivated by the social issues to rise above party. In his brief speech to the 1976 Republican National Convention, Reagan had specifically addressed not only "fellow Republicans," but "all those millions of Democrats and independents who I know are looking for a cause around which to rally, and which I believe we can give them." They rallied for Reagan and for Bush in 1988. Once in the Oval Office, however, Bush never reached out to them or addressed the issues they cared about. They went back to the Democratic Party and voted for Bill Clinton.

The 1992 convention was so peaceful that it afforded an opportunity for mischief-making. Mary Dent Crisp, the former co-chairman of the Republican National Committee who had left the party in 1980 to support John Anderson, had come back in 1989 but was threatening to leave again unless the party reversed its position on abortion. Crisp started the National Republican Coalition for Choice, and in 1990 the Republican fundraiser Ann Stone started another group, called Republicans for

Choice, a name she borrowed from a group that Planned Parenthood had started in 1982.

With easy access to the media, Crisp and Stone launched well-publicized threats to remove the pro-life plank from the Republican platform. The media were itching for something to liven up television coverage.

The Crisp-Stone faction played its trump card in Houston, triumphantly announcing that First Lady Barbara Bush wanted the pro-life plank ditched. The delegates who had worked hard to be elected to the platform committee, however, had minds of their own. The subcommittee on individual rights, good homes, and safe streets, chaired by Mary Potter Summa of North Carolina, conducted a dignified session with full debate, after which the vote was seventeen to three to retain the pro-life language of the 1984 and 1988 platforms. The pro-life plank was easily approved eighty-four to ten by the full platform committee. On the first day of the convention, the delegates adopted the platform on a unanimous voice vote.

The 1992 presidential election turned out to be a referendum on George Bush's presidency. The voters perceived Bush as running way from Ronald Reagan. Bush and his campaign team were condescending to Reagan Republicans and to Reagan Democrats. They were not in his policymaking loop or on his White House invitation list. His WASP administration kicked away the Catholic vote that had been an essential part of Reagan's victories. The Bush campaign excluded the Reagan conservatives, the pro-lifers, and the so-called religious right from important positions in his campaign.

Bush campaign strategists seemed to care more about who would control the party after the election than whether the election would be won, a typical attitude of country club Republicans. Bush avoided all the social issues that had been winners for him in 1988. Bush even went before a Christian Coalition audience on September 11, 1992, and spouted feminist ideology by making a disparaging reference to the "Ozzie and Harriet"–style family.

Immediately after George Bush was defeated by Bill Clinton in November 1992, powerful financial and media forces launched a propaganda campaign to rewrite the history of the 1992 election. The Establishment Republicans and their media friends saw in George Bush's defeat the opportunity to drive from party leadership the grassroots segments of the Republican Party that threatened their power. The Establishment was frightened at the possibility that the new coalition of fiscal and social conservatives who had twice elected Ronald Reagan might become dominant in the Republican Party.

Establishment Republicans care most of all about financial issues. They want large federal budgets and an interventionist foreign policy to conceal their corporate welfare and protect their foreign trade and overseas investments. As modern technology gives them the opportunity to extend their financial interests globally, they seek a new world economic order in which their interests are not restricted by inconvenient impediments such as national borders or what they call "outdated" concepts of sovereignty and patriotism. Country club Republicans want to drive out of all positions of political influence those who are motivated by the cultural issues, such as patriotism, respect for life, and family values. The political power of the pro-life movement threatens Establishment control of the party.

So after President Bush lost the election of 1992, an orchestrated propaganda campaign began to blame his defeat on pro-lifers and on those who had spoken about social and patriotic issues at the convention in Houston, notably Pat Buchanan and Dan and Marilyn Quayle. The truth is that the television networks' own public opinion polls conducted immediately after the convention showed that the Buchanan and Quayle convention speeches gave George Bush a big lift with the voters.

In the wake of Bush's defeat in 1992, Republicans asked themselves how was it possible that the Bush administration made so many mistakes. How could the governor of Arkansas, with so much embarrassing personal and financial baggage, defeat the incumbent president? Did Bush want to lose?

Of course Bush didn't want to lose. But his chief backers, the liberal Republican Establishment, cared more about keeping control of the Republican Party than about reelecting Bush, and they cared more about maintaining their access to taxpayer subsidies than about electing Republicans.

Well before the 1992 election, the financial crowd had established its ties to Rhodes scholar Bill Clinton. They knew he would pursue their big government and globalist agenda and carry out initiatives for their version of a "new world order."

The eager opportunist from Hope, Arkansas, was already a globalist and would be easy to adapt to their purposes. Clinton's education and patrons had enabled him to adopt the goals of the financially powerful who don't care which party one belongs to, just so long as an internationalist agenda is followed. Their spokesman, David Rockefeller Jr., announced their choice in an op-ed in the *New York Times* on October 16, 1992, titled "Why I Trust Clinton."

Bill Clinton was a college protégé of the Georgetown University professor Carroll Quigley, author of the 1,348-page book *Tragedy and Hope: A History of the World in Our Time* (1966), in which he revealed his personal acquaintance with the dynastic families of the super-rich. Quigley wrote in admiration of what he called the "network" of "international bankers" and other men who wield "the secret use of financial influence in political life." Quigley described the political conflict between grassroots Americans and the big financial interests as "the Midwest of Tom Sawyer against the cosmopolitan East of J. P. Morgan and Company."[1]

The "Hope" in Quigley's book title represents the collectivist one-world society that will exist after the "international Anglophile network" achieves its goal of consolidating its rule. He could hardly have anticipated that his Arkansas student would one day become president, but Quigley started Clinton on his climb to power by helping him to become a Rhodes scholar. When Clinton delivered his acceptance speech at the Democratic National Convention in New York City in 1992, he publicly credited Professor Carroll Quigley with helping to form his political outlook.

After Clinton moved into the White House, he outdid President John F. Kennedy in putting fellow Rhodes scholars in charge of U.S. policy.[2] Senator

John H. Chafee, a Rhode Island Republican, commented at a confirmation hearing in 1993, "They seem to be everywhere." Clinton may have looked like Tom Sawyer when he came out of Hope, but he learned fast how to make himself an errand boy for the cosmopolitan East.

As governor of Arkansas, Clinton had cultivated a profitable association with a Little Rock bank owned by the Riady family of Indonesia, a Chinese banking family that had some five billion dollars of business investments closely interlocked with the Chinese government, the Chinese Communist Party, and Chinese military intelligence. When battered by the Gennifer Flowers scandal in the spring of 1992, Clinton's faltering campaign received a multi-million dollar transfusion from the Riady Arkansas bank. Throughout 1992, millions of dollars of Riady money poured into states that were vital to Clinton's nomination and election.

After Clinton became president, he paid off the Riadys by giving their man in America, John Huang, a key job in the Commerce Department with top secret clearance. This gave Huang access to extremely sensitive CIA information of great value to the Riadys and their associates in Chinese intelligence. Clinton later moved Huang, with his security clearance intact, to the Democratic National Committee in order to strut his skills as a fundraiser for Clinton's television campaign for reelection.

Clinton announced in his 1996 State of the Union speech, "The era of big government is over. We know big government does not have all the answers. There is not a program for every problem." Having spoken those throwaway conservative lines to get audience cheers, Clinton implemented a laundry list of leftwing spending programs and advances toward socialist control of the economy and the public schools. We listened in vain for conservative Republican opposition.

Bipartisanship silenced Congress from curbing Clinton's blizzard of power-grabbing executive orders, his militarization of law enforcement, his implementation of unratified treaties, his incremental implementation of his discredited health care bill, and his attempts to build a Big Brother state in which the government monitors more and more of the daily activities of law-abiding Americans by databases of banking records, medical records, vaccine records, travel records, driver's licenses, cell phone calls and employment records. Social experimentation and feminization in the military proceeded at a rapid pace without protest from Republicans.

The most important political events of Bill Clinton's first term were the smashing Republican victory in the mid-term election of November 1994, when Republicans took over the House of Representatives for the first time in forty-two years, and the stunning defeat of the massive Hillary Clinton health care bill. Those victories encouraged grassroots Republicans to believe they could take back the White House in 1996.

23

The Dole Debacle

1996

I n mid-1995, the Washington establishment and press corps were toying with General Colin Powell as their number-one choice for president. The ultimate insider, Powell seemed the perfect candidate: he had spent his life taking orders and he could be depended on to do likewise in the White House. He was already using "new world order" lingo when he addressed the midshipmen at the Naval Academy in January 1993.

The buildup was orchestrated in the media. Powell appeared six times on the covers of *Time*, *Newsweek*, and *U.S. News & World Report*. Larry King, Barbara Walters, David Frost, Katie Couric, Tom Brokaw, and Jay Leno all invited him for televised chats. Powell's autobiography had all the earmarks of an expensively designed campaign piece for a presidential campaign.[1] Enthusiasts for Powell included some highly regarded conservative spokesmen, such as William Kristol, whose neoconservative magazine the *Weekly Standard* premiered with the prediction that Powell would be the Republican nominee. Former Secretary of Education William Bennett raised eyebrows when he signaled support for Powell despite Powell's non-Republican views on abortion, guns, and affirmative action.

Powellmania reached the apogee of its silliness in October 1995 when newspapers gleefully reported that *Burke's Peerage*, the British genealogical authority, discovered that Powell is "a direct descendant of the warrior King Edward I of England and a distant cousin of both Queen Elizabeth II and Princess Diana."

Being unfamiliar with party politics and the baggage carried by certain words, Powell made fatal mistakes in his early interviews. He identified himself as a "Rockefeller Republican," allowing the *New York Times* to give front-page coverage to what it called Powell's "emerging reputation as the political heir of Nelson A. Rockefeller."[2] Powell didn't realize that the very word "Rockefeller" is anathema to grassroots conservatives. Then he proclaimed himself "pro-choice," another radioactive term which, to grassroots Republicans, means killing unborn babies.

The *Washington Post* reporter Bob Woodward reported that after Powell watched the Conservative Political Action Conference on C-SPAN, Powell remarked, "Can you imagine me standing up and talking to these people?" Powell had apparently associated with the country club set for so many years that he had acquired their disdain for grassroots Republicans who labor in the precincts. "These people" did not appreciate such political snobbery.[3]

It didn't help Powell's candidacy when Ted Kennedy remarked on *Meet the Press* that Powell "talks a little more like a Democrat,"[4] or when the liberal Democratic Senator Paul Simon of Illinois speculated that Powell would be "a good choice" for President.

Conservatives rallied to nip Powell's candidacy in the bud. Paul Weyrich of the Free Congress Foundation told CNN's *Inside Politics*, "If he [Powell] should get the Republican nomination, it would be as if Ronald Reagan never lived and Nelson Rockefeller never died." The American Conservative Union's chairman, David Keene, added, "I cannot find any reason why any conservative would want to sacrifice the work of decades on the altar of celebrity." On November 2, 1995, Keene led a preemptive strike to cut off Powell's candidacy with a news conference at which thirteen conservative groups opposed Powell's candidacy for a variety of reasons.

On November 8, Powell announced he would not be a candidate for president. His Sherman-like statement even killed the Establishment's Plan B: to nominate Bob Dole for president with Colin Powell as his running mate.

As the 1996 presidential campaign got under-way, conservatives were divided among Phil Gramm, Patrick Buchanan, Steve Forbes, Alan Keyes, and Bob Dornan. In the early primaries, Buchanan inspired the sort of grassroots enthu-siasm that struck terror in the Establishment.

When Buchanan won an upset victory in the New Hampshire primary, the entire Establishment apparatus closed ranks to stop him. *Newsweek* featured a mean-looking picture of Buchanan on its cover, headlined "Preaching Fear." Colin Powell emerged from his self-imposed political silence to accuse Buchanan of "intolerance," and New York Mayor Rudolph Giuliani, who had up to then been neutral, proclaimed, "We're going to do everything we can to stop Buchanan." William Kristol thundered, "Someone needs to stand up and defend the establishment.… We at the *Weekly Standard* are pulling up the drawbridge against the peasants."

Bob Dole was a candidate with whom liberal Republicans could feel comfortable. He would go along on all the money and internationalist issues they cared about, and he wouldn't make any waves about the issues they didn't want to discuss.

Bob Dole was also exactly the kind of candidate Republican officeholders like. They are comfortable with a man who has been working for the government all his life. Since Congress lives by rules of seniority and the cult of incumbency, Bob Dole was next in line. George Will predicted that Dole would be nominated in 1996 because Republicans believe in primogeniture (the system in which the first-born inherits everything).

By mid-March, the media were regarding Bob Dole's nomination as inevitable and searching for some other controversy to make the 1996 Republican National Convention exciting. They began reporting that the convention would see a knock-down drag-out fight about the plank in the platform that recognizes "the fundamental individual right to life" of the unborn baby.

It was clear that the majority of 1996 delegates favored retaining the pro-life plank, which had been in the party platform ever since *Roe v. Wade* and in its current language since 1984. Many delegates were dedicated pro-lifers, and many others pragmatically recognized that the pro-life vote has become absolutely essential to Republican victories. Pro-lifers were a major segment of the coalition that produced Ronald Reagan's victories in 1980 and 1984, George Bush's victory in 1988, and the Republican congressional victory of 1994.

During the spring and summer of 1996, Dole repeatedly shot himself in the foot on the abortion issue. He had promised his pro-abortion supporters that he would either get rid of or water down the pro-life plank. On June 10 Dole stated on CNN that a "tolerance" statement is "going to be in the abortion plank," adding, "I make that decision. It's not negotiable." Dole apparently didn't know that the nominee for president can no longer dictate the Republican platform as Nixon and Rockefeller dictated it in 1960. The platform is written by a committee consisting of one man and one woman elected from each state. Republicans who work hard to be elected to the platform committee take their responsibilities seriously.

The 1996 platform committee treated the pro-abortionists courteously and allowed them plenty of time to make their arguments, but the largest number of votes they received was eleven out of 107, a decline from the sixteen they had received at the 1992 convention in Houston. Eleven was not even enough to file a minority report.

The committee wrote a conservative, pro-life platform that was unanimously adopted by the full convention on August 12. Bob Dole then insulted the delegates by announcing to the press, "I haven't read the platform and I'm not bound by it anyway." The party managers excised the social, cultural, and sovereignty issues from Dole's campaign. Bob Dole personally demanded that one paragraph be added to the party platform, and the committee included it:

> We are the party of the open door.... We view this diversity of views as a source of strength, not a sign of weakness, and we welcome into our ranks all Americans who may hold differing positions. We are committed to resolving our differences in a spirit of civility, hope, and mutual respect.

Everyone agreed to that paragraph, but the Dole convention managers soon made it crystal clear that the concepts of "open door," "diversity," welcoming "differing positions," "civility," and "mutual respect" applied only to pro-abortion and Rockefeller Republicans, not to Buchananites.

In one of the most curious Dole dictates, none of the other presidential candidates—Phil Gramm, Pat Buchanan, Bob Dornan, Alan Keyes, or Steve Forbes—was allowed to address the convention. Customarily, a winning candidate makes immediate overtures to the candidates he defeated in the primaries, hoping to get their supporters' votes in the general election.

The people managing Dole's campaign were far more interested in consolidating their control of the Republican Party than in putting Bob Dole in the White House. Excluding all the really dynamic Republican speakers made the San Diego convention boring, and television ratings were the lowest ever.

Dole himself didn't believe in Republican diversity. On the day after Buchanan won the New Hampshire primary, Dole personally stuck in the knife and twisted it by saying, "This now is a race between the mainstream and the extreme, that's what it's all about." Two days later, he rebuffed conservative leaders who asked him to soft-pedal his rhetoric. In describing himself as "mainstream" and Buchanan as "extreme," Dole reintroduced into political discourse the same words that Nelson Rockefeller used against Barry Goldwater in 1964. The epithet "extreme" continues to be used against conservatives by the Democrats and the media.

The delegates were treated like stage props for a television show, not like participants in a live convention. Special techniques were used to keep delegates in their place. Loud music blared incessantly, making conversation difficult. There was no diversity in the music—no patriotic numbers, no state songs, no John Philip Sousa, just deafening rock music to drown out the delegates. No signs were allowed to enter the hall except officially issued Dole or Dole-Kemp signs. The 1996 Republican National Convention in San Diego was so tightly controlled that Alan Keyes labeled it a "Stalinist convention."

Spontaneous demonstrations have always been one of the most exciting interactive events at national political conventions, but there was none in San Diego. Hundreds of young people were brought in to stand in the aisles to keep delegates from walking around to visit other delegations or participate in demonstrations. Confined to assigned rows of seats, delegates could only sit, stand in place, hold up a Dole-Kemp sign, and wiggle.

A Dole whip was assigned to each state delegation. He received his orders through his earpiece and transmitted prompts to the delegates to whom he was assigned. He told delegates when to stand up, when to sit down, when to hold up their signs and wiggle, what to yell in response to speakers' rhetorical questions, and when to chant "Dole-Kemp, Dole-Kemp." The ugliest manifestation of dictatorial control occurred on Wednesday night, August 14, during the roll-call vote for president. In the 1996 primaries, Pat Buchanan had won about 143 delegates and made big national news when he won the New Hampshire primary. But when the votes were cast that night, Buchanan received only forty-three votes and none from New Hampshire! What happened to the missing one hundred votes? The national news media did not assign any investigative reporter to discover the perpetrators of this theft.

The Dole managers issued orders that Buchanan's name was not to be mentioned over the convention microphones, and they went to unprecedented lengths to enforce that order. First, Dole agents tried to intimidate Buchanan delegates into switching their votes to Dole "in the name of party unity." Some delegates agreed. Strong-arm tactics were applied to those who were not going along. Some states were told to invoke a "unit rule," by which the majority of a state's delegation casts 100 percent of the state's votes—even though that is prohibited by Republican convention rules. Some states were told that delegates could not cast a vote for someone whose name had not been officially placed in nomination. That too is a violation of convention rules.

After all but one of Buchanan's New Hampshire delegates had been intimidated into switching their votes to Dole, the lone holdout, a very pregnant woman, was cruelly harassed and reduced to tears by being told that, if she didn't vote for Dole, New Hampshire would lose its first-in-the-nation primary, the state would lose millions of dollars, and it would be her fault.

The ten Buchanan delegates from Louisiana were the target of particularly heavy pressure. They were threatened that their Republican candidate for the U.S. Senate, Woody Jenkins, would not get any national funds unless all Buchanan delegates switched to Dole. When the roll call reached Louisiana, a large group of young men carrying Dole-Kemp signs surrounded that state's delegates to hide them from the television cameras.

The Dole managers forbade the states to announce the votes Buchanan had won in the primaries. This was accomplished either by giving orders to the state delegation chairmen *not* to announce the Buchanan votes or by cutting off the microphones before any Buchanan votes could be announced. Thus, the convention secretary, Kay James, solemnly intoned, "Alaska, nineteen votes." The Alaska chairman responded, Alaska "casts sixteen votes for Bob Dole." There was no mention of the other three votes.

The secretary continued the roll call: "Arizona, thirty-nine votes," and Arizona responded, "Thirty-seven for Bob Dole." Silence followed. Where were the other two votes? The secretary continued: "Arkansas, twenty votes," and Arkansas responded, "Sixteen votes for Bob Dole." No mention of the other four votes. "Idaho, twenty-three votes." Idaho answered, "Nineteen votes for Bob Dole." Nobody asked about the missing four votes. "North Dakota, eighteen votes," and North Dakota responded, "Seventeen votes for Bob Dole." The missing vote was not accounted for.

The Dole people couldn't budge Missouri, the Show-Me State, which succeeded in casting eleven of its thirty-six votes for Buchanan, because the delegates were prepared to resist the pressure. But when the roll call reached Missouri, the entire bloc of one hundred New York delegates stood up so Missouri could not be seen by the television cameras.

The Buchanan delegates whose votes were stolen were weeping and angry, but they didn't have the microphones. Gone were the days when a delegate could demand that his state's delegation be publicly polled in order to flush out the truth.

At the end of the roll call, the Convention Chairman announced, "The vote is concluded," but he did not announce the tally. It may have been the only election in history where the total vote count was not announced. The chairman immediately recognized a motion to declare the vote for Bob Dole "unanimous." When the *Official Report of the Proceedings of the 1996 Republican National Convention* was printed, it conspicuously omitted the tally of that first ballot.

What difference could it make to Bob Dole whether he got 1,990 votes on the roll call or 1,890 votes? But the Establishment manipulators would tolerate no dissent because their goal was to solidify their control of the party, not to win elections. It was simply unacceptable—"politically incorrect," if you will—to be a non-Dole delegate. The Establishment made sure they controlled the gavel, the microphones, the rules committee, the credentials committee, the agenda, the aisles, the signs, the band, the telephones, the communication system, the chairmenships of state delegations, hundreds of paid whips, the sergeants at arms, and the big New York and California delegations.

Dole's defeat in the November election cannot be blamed on any social or cultural issues because Dole and Kemp never talked about them. Dole's campaign was classic me-tooism. Exactly like past Establishment candidates, Dole and Kemp failed to campaign on their best issues. Bob Dole never addressed social or cultural issues during his campaign or TV debates. On October 9, the *New York Times* ran a front-page news story headlined "Dole Still Silent On Major Issues." The newspaper expressed bewilderment that Dole failed to use the social issues—abortion (including Clinton's veto of the popular partial-birth abortion ban), affirmative action, immigration, welfare—issues that the *Times* stated would "drive President Clinton to the left and ultimately off the edge of the electoral map."

When Republican candidates talk only about economic issues, they reinforce the stereotype—completely false, but unfortunately believed by many people—that Republicans care only about money, while Democrats care about people.

The media praised the nationally televised debates in the fall of 1996, two presidential and one vice presidential, for their civility. But that very civility gave voters the impression that there wasn't any particular difference between the candidates. A majority (51 percent) of voting-age Americans chose *not* to vote in the presidential election, the lowest turnout since 1924. The voters resigned themselves to enduring four more years of a man they didn't trust. They saw no reason to replace him with a man whose policies were not significantly different.

Contrary to the postmortems by Dole apologists, Clinton's reelection in November 1996 was not inevitable. He had two serious vulnerabilities—people didn't trust his character and he was more liberal than Dole. Voters never willingly choose the more untrustworthy or the more liberal candidate. Dole didn't make the case on either issue.

Bill Clinton's reelection can be blamed on all the people who insisted that Bob Dole be the Republican nominee. That includes his financial backers, officeholders, and the corporate lobbyists who all knew Dole personally and had to know what a poor candidate he would be. How could anyone expect that Dole would make an acceptable president when he agreed with Bill Clinton on most issues and wouldn't talk about the issues on which they disagreed?

After Bill Clinton was reelected in 1996, he began to unfold his plans for global governance. In a speech to the United Nations General Assembly on September 22, 1997, Clinton called the series of treaties he was promoting a "web of institutions and arrangements" that set "the international ground rules for the 21st century." He urged Americans to support what he called "the emerging international system."

His metaphor "web" was apt. He specified the treaties by which he wanted to enmesh us in a global network: the World Trade Organization, the Chemical Weapons Convention, "binding international commitments to protect the environment" (i.e., the Kyoto Protocol), and the NATO Expansion Treaty.

No one should have been surprised at the scope of Clinton's global ambitions. They reflected the thinking of all his foreign policy advisers. His Oxford roommate and chief adviser on Russia, Strobe Talbott, wrote for *Time* magazine for twenty-two years. In a July 20, 1992, article entitled "The Birth of the Global Nation," Talbott enthusiastically predicted that in the next century, "Nationhood as we know it will be obsolete, all states will recognize a single, global authority." "National sovereignty wasn't such a great idea after all," Talbott assured *Time*'s readers.[5]

24

Follow the Big Money

2000

A s Republicans contemplated the end of two terms of Bill Clinton, they dreamed of electing a genuine private enterprise conservative such as Steve Forbes. Bob Dole dashed cold water on that hope. "[T]he Establishment has decided it's going to be [George W.] Bush," Dole pontificated on Chris Matthews's *Hardball* in late 1999.

By the year 2000, New York was no longer the center of political power. The Chase Manhattan Bank crowd was nowhere in sight. It was no longer sufficient for the kingmakers to huddle in a New York hotel room or pay Madison Avenue to "sell" their candidate or to hire perpetrators of dirty tricks along the campaign trail. The globalists had consolidated their influence over the leadership of both political parties, and cold hard cash was the only thing that mattered.

When the political power brokers gathered to anoint a candidate for president, it wasn't difficult to settle on Texas Governor George W. Bush. After all, he was next in line, and he could probably be counted on to continue his father's internationalist policies. By the time Bob Dole made his prediction, he could see that money would not be a problem for George W. Bush.

Bush quickly learned how to generate enormous sums of political money. He shattered all records by collecting over a hundred million dollars from individuals. At least a third of those funds was raised by his 214 "Pioneers," each of whom raised at least a hundred thousand dollars, and his "Rangers," each raising two hundred thousand. Small groups of bankers and corporate tycoons were flying to Austin for private lunches at the Texas governor's mansion. Michael Isikoff labeled them "potential kingmakers" and quoted political experts as being "awed" by Bush's "phenomenal" money machine.

Bush also knew how to cut off the flow of money to his competitors, as former Vice President Dan Quayle quickly discovered when he started to telephone Republican donors. Journalist Howard Fineman reported, "In 2000, the Bush family made sure that the message went out: if you are a friend of ours, we want you to give *only* to our boy. Sure, Dan Quayle had been Bush One's Veep, but don't give him any money."

In January 2000, a majority of Republican National Committee members endorsed George W. Bush, the first time so many RNC members had ever endorsed a presidential candidate so early in a contested nomination process. About the same time, twenty-five of the thirty-one GOP governors endorsed him.

Corporate money was on vulgar display in a two-page ad in the *New York Times* on February 11, 1999. A long list of officials from the Gerald Ford and George H. W. Bush administrations joined with powerful CEOs to sign a two-page demand that Congress immediately vote for four of Bill Clinton's goals: (1) more tax handouts to the International Monetary Fund, (2) use of the Exchange Stabilization Fund to prop up foreign currencies, (3) payment of one billion dollars in "back dues" to the United Nations, and (4) fast-track trade authority for Clinton. Republican signers of these demands included Gerald Ford, former secretaries of state Henry Kissinger and Alexander Haig, former national security advisors Brent Scowcroft and Robert McFarlane, former U.S. trade representatives Bill Brock and Carla Hills, and the heads of scores of multinational corporations and banks.

The corporate elite were even more conspicuous when they traveled to Shanghai on September 27, 1999, to pay homage to the Chinese Communist Party on the occasion of the fiftieth anniversary of its takeover of mainland China. The U.S. delegation was impressive: the CEOs of hundreds of *Fortune* 500 corporations, including Time-Warner, General Motors, Ford, AT&T, Procter and Gamble, Boeing, Rockwell, and Cargill. On hand to provide helpful tips were those experienced global travelers Henry Kissinger and Carla Hills (Republicans) and Robert Rubin and Mickey Kantor (Democrats).

President Clinton's national security adviser, Samuel R. "Sandy" Berger, was assigned to deliver the kingmakers' foreign policy strategy for the 2000 election regardless of which party was elected. It was neatly summed up in the title of his address: "Strengthening the Bipartisan Center: An Internationalist Agenda for America." His speech defined the "internationalist agenda," asserted that "bipartisanism" is the road to take us there, and warned that "isolationism" is the dragon to be slain along the way. Aren't sovereignty and national independence outdated concepts? Isn't the function of government to provide taxpayer subsidies for global trade and to ensure that poorly educated public school alumni compete in the low-wage global economy?

To give this message to the movers and shakers of the world, Sandy Berger arrived in a White House limousine at the Library of Congress on the evening of November 4, 1999. In the magnificent Great Hall of the Jefferson Building, he addressed a dinner gathering of the steering committee of the Bilderberg Group, the association of European and North American political and business elites. David Rockefeller, Vernon Jordan Jr., and Henry Kissinger were on hand to host the guests.

There was no secret about Berger's speech to the Bilderbergers; the Clinton administration posted it on the White House website. Clinton was cocky enough to assure the international community that Republican leaders had been coopted into continuing Clinton's foreign policies.

Three weeks after Sandy Berger's speech to the Bilderbergers, Condoleezza Rice made clear that she was incorporating Bill Clinton's foreign policy as defined by Sandy Berger into George W. Bush's policy. She announced on ABC, "He will bring a new Bipartisan Center to American foreign policy."[1]

It was well known that Condoleezza Rice had been engaged to be George W. Bush's chief foreign policy adviser. She had already take a leave of absence from her job at Stanford University to gather a team to brief Bush on foreign policy. This group called themselves Vulcans, named after the big statue in Birmingham, Alabama, Rice's home town.

When it became apparent that important businessmen had preselected the Republican nominee, a fault line appeared among the kingmakers. The media kingmakers responded with a candidate of their own: Senator John McCain. The media jumped on his bandwagon because they were enthusiastic about his campaign finance limitation proposals. His plan would prohibit donations from non-media corporations and severely limit the donations of their executives but would allow unlimited endorsements and coverage by media corporations. From the media's perspective, that was win-win. McCain's ties to the media were reinforced by his chairmanship of the Senate subcommittee on telecommunications.

The Bush-McCain battle in the Republican primaries became a contest of titans: the corporate establishment versus the media establishment. Bush's giant head start in fundraising was challenged by an estimated hundred million dollars in free media showered on McCain.

McCain's campaign picked up a life of its own. He acquired a following of people attracted by the image of a macho leader with overtones of heroism. He also attracted an anti-establishment constituency of those who resented the way party bigwigs had inflicted on Republicans the failed campaigns of Bush the father and Bob Dole and then greased the process for Bush the son. The media were happy about the Bush-McCain contest because it engendered no real foreign policy debate. Both supported the Clinton-Albright war against Serbia.

McCain's campaign made it clear that a candidate does not have to be pro-choice to attract moderates and independents to vote Republican. McCain presented himself as pro-life and pledged that he would seek no change in the pro-life plank of the Republican platform.

Things were going well for the insurgent McCain, but on the way to his hoped-for upset victory, he made a major miscalculation. He apparently thought he could do what the Rockefeller wing of the Republican Party has been itching to do ever since the glory days of Ronald Reagan's victories, namely, cut the clout of the so-called religious right. Of course, the media could be counted on to support a frontal assault.

After piously pontificating against negative ads, McCain went to Virginia Beach and made a mean-spirited attack on Pat Robertson and Jerry Falwell, calling them "agents of intolerance." This played well with the media, who want to drive the Christian conservatives back into their pews, but Christian conservatives are far too numerous and dynamic to be exorcised. McCain suffered major primary defeats on Super Tuesday and folded his campaign on March 9.

So the nomination of George W. Bush was locked up before the Republican National Convention convened in Philadelphia in July 2000. It was even preordained that Dick Cheney would be his running mate.

Most of the grassroots believed that George W. Bush would restore dignity, conservatism, and even Reaganism to the White House. The platform adopted in Philadelphia included the following:

> We support the traditional definition of marriage as the legal union of one man and one woman.... The unborn baby has a fundamental individual right to life.... We do not believe sexual preference should be given special legal protection in law....We stand with the Boy Scouts of America, and support their positions.... We oppose euthanasia and assisted suicide.... We defend the constitutional right to keep and bear arms....We support the recognition of English as the nation's common language.... We affirm the right of public schools, courthouses, and other public buildings to post copies

> of the Ten Commandments.... [We support the appointment of] judges who have demonstrated that they share . . . conservative beliefs and respect the Constitution.... We support a national missile defense.... American troops must never serve under U.N. command or be subject to the jurisdiction of an International Criminal Court.

The pro-abortion minority in the Republican Party staged its usual tantrums to get media coverage, but they were not successful in eliminating the pro-life plank of the platform.

The grassroots were so hungry to win back the White House after two terms of Bill Clinton that they were willing to tolerate Bush's deviations from conservative orthodoxy on many issues, but not on the sanctity of life. When the pro-abortion governor of Pennsylvania, Tom Ridge, was floated as a possible running mate for Bush, I easily quashed that bad idea by telling the *New York Times,* "He'd lose if he did that."

After the liberals failed to defeat Bush in the 2000 election and failed to defeat him in the recount and in Al Gore's appeal to the courts, the liberals launched a campaign to challenge his legitimacy, or as Charles Krauthammer described it, "to neuter him" by demanding that he be a bipartisan president.

George W. Bush did walk the walk of bipartisanship. The overriding strategy of his administration was forecast by his foreign policy guru, Condoleezza Rice, who had promised, echoing Sandy Berger's speech to the Bilderbergers, that Bush would bring "a new Bipartisan Center to American foreign policy." On July 29, 2001, she said on CBS's *Face the Nation*, "You will not find a more internationalist administration than this administration." The 2000 presidential campaigns produced no national debate on the issues that would determine the survival of America as a free and independent nation. Any candidate who talked about his opponents' records was accused of "negative campaigning."

Bill Clinton's mentor, Professor Carroll Quigley, had explained in *Tragedy and Hope* that the Bipartisan Center is the Establishment's longtime goal:

> The argument that the two parties should represent opposed ideals and policies, one, perhaps, of the Right and the other of the Left, is a foolish idea....
>
> Instead the two parties should be almost identical, so that the American people can "throw the rascals out" at any election without leading to any profound or extensive shifts in policy. The [Eastern Establishment] policies that are vital and

> necessary for America are no longer sub-
> jects of significant disagreement, but are
> disputable only in details of procedure,
> priority or method.

Once George W. Bush was in the White House, he tried to remold the conservative movement as "compassionate conservatism." Conservatives began to see that phrase not only as a sly innuendo that conservatism was not already compassionate but as a euphemism for big government. Citing Bush's position on spending, immigration, and campaign finance, Judge Robert Bork commented, "This George Bush, like his father, is showing himself to be indifferent, if not actively hostile, to conservative values."

George W. Bush expanded the Department of Education farther than the Democrats could have hoped and invited Senator Ted Kennedy to help draft the thousand-page No Child Left Behind bill. It boasted a price tag of eight billion dollars more than the last Clinton education bill. Senator Paul Wellstone, a Democrat from Minnesota, described it as "a stunning federal mandate" that strikes at "the essence of local control." Bush's White House even lobbied against parental option for the bilingual education mandate in No Child Left Behind. Calling himself "a uniter, not a divider,"

Bush renamed the FBI headquarters the Robert F. Kennedy Building.

Trying to appease the feminists, the Bush administration reaffirmed irrational feminist regulations under Title IX of the Education Act—anti-male, anti-masculine regulations that now appear to be permanent.

Bush turned to Ted Kennedy time and again to push the biggest items on his domestic agenda: education, prescription drugs, and immigration. The Bush administration's lobbying for the Medicare prescription drug bill in November 2003 shocked even old-timers who were used to hardball tactics. Conservative Republicans were browbeaten into voting for the bill by promises of funding (or threats of withholding funding) for their next campaign, threats of a primary challenge, or ostracism from party leadership. Even though he had just returned from Europe, President Bush made personal phone calls at four o'clock in the morning to bring the last two congressmen into line before the vote.

When RNC Chairman Ed Gillespie went to New Hampshire in August 2003, he defined "fiscal responsibility" to mean that federal spending would increase at "a slower rate of growth" than if the Democrats were in power. George W. Bush ran his campaign without calling for a single spending cut or the elimination of any program, agency, or department. The *Manchester Union Leader* concluded that "the days of Reaganesque Republican railings against the expansion of federal government are over." By the end of 2003, the *New York Times* proclaimed:

> The Republican Party has been in charge of the national agenda for almost three years now.... The most striking thing about the new Republicanism is the way it embraces big government. The Bush administration has presided over a $400 billion expansion of Medicare entitlements. The party that once campaigned to abolish the Department of Education has produced an education plan that involves unprecedented federal involvement in local public schools.

Bush's style of governance was markedly different from his predecessors'. He valued loyalty above competence and surrounded himself with obsequious courtiers. His first choices for the most important appointments a president can make, Supreme Court justices, were persons whose only qualification was personal friendship. Whereas George H. W. Bush had relied on establishment pedigree in making his appointments, and Bill Clinton preferred academic credentials,

George W. Bush's appointment strategy was to reward the men and women who were his friends, a practice called cronyism.

It was widely known that Bush hoped to use his first Supreme Court vacancy to appoint the first Hispanic to the Court, his personal lawyer, Alberto Gonzales. Conservatives killed that speculation after Gonzales admitted in a public forum that he would uphold *Roe v. Wade* and that the president could take us into war without a vote by Congress. This joke made the rounds in Washington: How do you say Souter in Spanish? Gonzales.

Bush's second choice was Harriet Miers, a feminist with no qualifications for the Supreme Court and who had never written anything about the U.S. Constitution. Conservatives across the spectrum from Bill Kristol to Pat Buchanan rallied to quash Bush's choice, and the fortunate result was the confirmation of Samuel Alito.

Some of the issues that were not discussed or debated during the presidential campaign included Clinton's unconstitutional use of power to make war, the misuse of American military as global social workers in faraway lands, the feminization of the U.S. armed services, accepting jurisdiction of the International Criminal Court, and Clinton's three hundred power-grabbing executive orders.

On the other hand, Bush succeeded in getting Congress to pass his important tax cuts, which launched a significant improvement in the economy, and he took four significant actions that were not on the internationalists' agenda. (1) When the United Nations in July 2001 called for a worldwide ban on guns, Bush sent word that the United States would have no part of any plan to register or confiscate guns. (2) Bush gave formal notice to Russia in December 2001 that the United States was withdrawing from the thirty-year-old Anti-Ballistic Missile Treaty, which was negotiated by Henry Kissinger and signed by President Nixon as part of the 1972 SALT I agreements. Conservatives who believe in peace through strength had been calling for withdrawal from the ABM Treaty for more than twenty-five years. (3) Bush resisted all pressures to ratify Al Gore's favorite international agreement, the global warming treaty known as the Kyoto Protocol. (4) Bush sent a letter to U.N. Secretary General Kofi Annan in May 2002 revoking the United States' signature to the International Criminal Court Treaty, which Bill Clinton had signed just before midnight on New Year's Eve, 2000. Bush subsequently signed legislation authorizing military action if the ICC ever arrested an American.

The contest between George W. Bush and Al Gore was aptly described by William Safire's phrase the

"Gorebush Era," a situation that "fuzzies up legiti-
mate debate about ideology" and leaves us with a
choice between personalities and campaign styles.
Newsweek morphed Bush and Gore into one face
for its post-election cover. George W. Bush had done
just enough to keep his constituency revved up to
support his reelection.

25

Seeking a New World Order

2004

O f course the renomination of George W. Bush at the 2004 Republican National Convention in New York City was not controversial. The only surprise was the unprecedented, dictatorial way his people dictated the party platform.

The platform committee consists of one man and one woman from each state and territory, all of whom must first be elected as delegates and then elected by their fellow delegates to serve on the committee. Since this process is generally democratic, the platform committee has customarily had a comfortable majority of grassroots Republicans whose votes cannot be bought and who cannot be intimidated by party bosses.

The 2004 convention in New York City was quite different. President Bush sent orders to Republican state chairmen to allow on the platform committee only public or party officials who could be counted on to vote as they were instructed. About 90 percent of the platform committee members fitted that description. No platform committee hearings were held for citizens and experts to testify for or against resolutions. The time allotted for subcommittee and committee deliberations was reduced to about half the time of previous years.

Senator Bill Frist, the platform committee chairman, presided in the Jacob J. Javits Center in a high-handed way, gaveling down any plank that Bush didn't want, particularly on immigration and stem-cell research. It was widely believed that Frist's job as platform committee chairman was to be a stepping stone to his own presidential campaign in 2008, but that didn't happen.

Traditional platform committee procedure called for starting with a reception on Sunday evening, the week before the convention opens. The subcommittees would engage in serious deliberations on Monday and Tuesday, move to full committee consideration on Wednesday, and complete the work on Thursday or Friday. In 2004, the powers that be didn't dare to allow that much time even to their tightly controlled committee. The opening reception at which platform committee members were given their first look at the pre-written document was on Tuesday evening, August 24. The 2004 schedule called for subcommittees to meet only on Wednesday, with the final draft buttoned down by the full committee on Thursday.

Journalists commented on the "authorization aura" that kept the Bush draft of the platform as secret as the Manhattan Project and then saw it handed it down from on high like the Ten Commandments. George W. Bush was lauded on eighty-nine pages of the ninety-eight-page platform.[1]

The tight control and demand for Bush orthodoxy came from the Oval Office. Bush has a thirst for control and for secrecy. A *Washington Post* analysis quoted a former White House official as saying, "On all levels, the administration in Term 2 is promoting people who owe their careers to this president—people are forced to be loyal."

Pro-lifers were so strong in 2004 that President Bush knew it was expedient not to tamper with the pro-life plank, so he went along with its retention in the same language that had been in the platform since 1984. Delegates were not allowed to add strong planks on other issues except for some excellent language against judicial activism. The platform called on Congress to use its Article III power to withdraw jurisdiction from the federal courts over the Pledge of Allegiance, the Ten Commandments, and the Defense of Marriage Act, and quoted Bush as saying, "We will not stand for judges who undermine democracy by legislating from the bench and try to remake America by court order."

A couple of curiosities about the 2004 presidential campaign should be noted, although they made no difference in the outcome. Out of three hundred million American people, both presidential candidates, George W. Bush and John Kerry, were members of a tiny exclusive club based at Yale University called Skull and Bones that had perhaps only eight hundred living members. On February 8, 2004, on *Meet the Press*, Tim Russert baited Bush with the query, "You were both in Skull and Bones, the secret society." Bush replied, "It's so secretive we can't talk about it." It was unusual that Russert abstained from his usual aggressive follow-up.

The *New York Times* credited John Edwards' speech to the Bilderberg meeting in Stresa, Italy, in June 2004 as the key factor in his being chosen by the Democratic Party as John Kerry's running mate. A friend of Kerry's who attended that meeting of those powerful internationalists "reported back directly to Kerry" about Edwards' "performance at Bilderberg."[2]

Bush was fortunate to draw John Kerry as his opponent. According to Bob Novak, Kerry was a terrible candidate and was saddled with a billionaire wife who didn't know how to keep her mouth shut. But the mainstream media recognized his decisive margin of victory—3.3 million votes—as a mandate for genuine conservatism. The GOP increased its majority in the Senate from fifty-one to fifty-five and strengthened its hold on the House. The *New York Times* concluded that "it is impossible to read President Bush's re-election with larger Republican majorities in both Houses of Congress as anything other than the clearest confirmation yet that this is a center-right country."

Then, Bush's Second Inaugural Address on January 20, 2005, shocked his supporters:

> The survival of liberty in our land increasingly depends on the success of liberty in other lands. The best hope for peace in our world is the expansion of freedom in all the world.... It is the policy of the United States to seek and support the growth of democratic movements and institutions in every nation and culture, with the ultimate goal of ending tyranny in our world.... We go

forward with complete confidence in the eventual triumph of freedom.

Bush's aides spent the next week trying to explain what this speech meant. It could not be reconciled with his explicit pre-election promise *not* to engage in nation-building. In his debate against Al Gore in October 2000, Bush had declared, "I mean, are we going to have some kind of nation-building corps from America? Absolutely not."

George W. Bush's Second Inaugural Address signaled his switch from a foreign policy to protect the United States to the adoption of a massive U.S. mission of "ending tyranny in our world" and establishing universal democracy. His speech was short on specifics and substance but full of Wilsonian platitudes about freedom and democracy.

Bush had convinced himself that he could bestow freedom and stabilize the Middle East by the forcible removal of a tyrant and his party. Bush seemed to think that everyone in the world desires freedom above all. Unfortunately, that isn't true. Some people desire power above all, some revenge, and some simply civil order. So, under George W. Bush, nation-building moved from pejorative to priority. The U.S. Army's field manual was revised to put military post-conflict "stability operations" on a par with fighting wars.

The publisher of *Congressional Quarterly,* Robert W. Merry, explained in his book *Sands of Empire* that Bush's global ambitions were based on combining the moralism of Woodrow Wilson (to make the world "safe for democracy") and the exceptionalism of Theodore Roosevelt. Conservatives were starting to get nervous. In May 2005, the Senate Intelligence Committee chairman, Pat Roberts of Kansas, paid tribute to Bush for his courage after 9/11 but added, "We need to restrain what are growing U.S. messianic instincts—a sort of global social engineering where the United States feels it is both entitled and obligated to promote democracy—by force, if necessary." He called for "some hard-headed assessment of American interests." Representative John J. Duncan Jr., a Republican from Tennessee, complained that "Conservatives have never believed that the United States should be the policeman of the world."

George W. Bush had revealed himself as a thoroughgoing internationalist. One of the first things he did in his new term was to travel to Quebec to promote the Free Trade Area of the Americas, calling for economic integration of the entire Western Hemisphere. Conservatives quickly defeated that foolish idea.

Then, on March 23, 2005, Bush went to Waco, Texas, where he announced the Security and

Prosperity Partnership (SPP) of the United States, Canada, and Mexico. He was joined there by President Vicente Fox of Mexico and Prime Minister Paul Martin of Canada, and they became known as the "Three Amigos."

On May 17, 2005, the Council on Foreign Relations published a report explaining that the Three Amigos had "committed their governments" to "building a North American Community" by 2010 with a common "outer security perimeter," "the extension of full labor mobility to Mexico," allowing Mexican trucks "unlimited access," "totalization" of illegal aliens into the U.S. Social Security system, and a "permanent tribunal for North American dispute resolution."

The Hudson Institute followed with a 2007 white paper called "Negotiating North America: The Security and Prosperity Partnership." It stated that SPP is the vehicle "for economic integration" of the United States with Mexico and Canada. The Hudson report explained that SPP was designed to be "fully within the authority of the executive branch in the United States," and thereby evade treaty ratification and congressional oversight. The arrogance of this approach—an executive claim of full "authority" to "enforce and execute" whatever was decided by the "civil service professionals" of three nations—was exceeded only by its unconstitutionality.

At the North American Summit in Montebello, Quebec, on August 21, 2007, Fox News reporter Bret Baier asked all three leaders, "Can you say today that this is not a prelude to a North American Union, similar to a European Union?" None of the three denied that SPP is leading to a North American Union. Bush insulted the questioners by accusing them of believing in a "conspiracy." The North American Union gambit was so antagonistic to American patriotism, as well as unconstitutional, that we killed that plan, too.

In speeches to the National Endowment for Democracy in Washington and at Whitehall Palace in London in November 2003, he called for a "commitment to the global expansion of democracy" as "the alternative to instability and to hatred and terror" and as the "third pillar of our security."

By the end of George W. Bush's second term, conservatives' disappointment with him was deep and pervasive. The grassroots had to face the fact that Bush didn't behave like a conservative on the role of the federal government in war and peace, on spending, on education, on health policy, or on immigration. Maybe he wasn't a conservative after all.

Bush asked conservatives to take positions that they didn't believe in and that were contrary to their nature, their history, and their principles: support a war of interventionism, support expanded federal control of education, and add an extravagant new entitlement. With Harriet Miers, he trivialized the most important appointment he could make. He ignored leaders of the conservative movement and he displayed a shocking lack of concern for congressional Republicans' reelection prospects.

Bush turned off large segments of his own constituency by his advocacy of amnesty for illegal aliens and his failure to secure our borders or enforce existing immigration laws. It became clear that his trade policies were undermining our manufacturing base and sending millions of American jobs overseas. No Child Left Behind produced no improvement in public schools. Bush's energy policy allowed a tripling of the price of energy. The Iraq war did not bring democracy or peace to the Middle East, and the war on terror did not reduce the threat of Muslim terrorism. The columnist Robert Novak explained Republican losses in the congressional elections of 2006:

> Under George W. Bush, the Reaganite agenda of fighting Soviet imperialism abroad and starving government at home has been transformed into a Wilsonian desire to reform—to democratize—the world. Americans want to protect them-

selves from terrorists, but they clearly are not willing to pay any price to spread democracy around the world. They made that clear in voting on November 7.

When Bush unveiled his $2.57 trillion budget for 2006, people remembered that President Bill Clinton had said, "The era of big government is over." What happened? Bush boasted to his speechwriter Matt Latimer, "Look, I know this probably sounds arrogant to say, but I redefined the Republican Party."[3]

David Brooks described George W. Bush's attitude and rationale in the *New York Times*:

His self-confidence survives because it flows from two sources. The first is his unconquerable faith in the rightness of his Big Idea. Bush is convinced that history is moving in the direction of democracy.... Second, Bush remains energized by the power of the presidency.... Bush clearly loves the presidency.

Was this a change in Bush's concept of his mission, or had he all along planned to pursue a New World Order or a North American Union? One clue came from the post-administration writings of Michael Gerson, Bush's senior speech writer and political advisor from 2001 to 2006. Gerson's own beliefs became known to the American people only after he left the administration to write for the *Washington Post* and *Newsweek* and to serve as a senior fellow at the Council on Foreign Relations. In his columns, Gerson revealed that he nurtured significant dislike of traditional conservatism. He repeatedly criticized conservatives, comparing skeptics of Bush's comprehensive immigration bill to nativist bigots of the 1880s. He wrote approvingly of Franklin D. Roosevelt and Jimmy Carter, while disdaining Friedrich Hayek and Ludwig von Mises.

26

Fundamentally Transforming America

2008

The 2008 presidential campaign got underway early in 2007, since many states had advanced the dates of their primary to try to diminish what they perceived as the undue importance of the Iowa caucuses and the New Hampshire primary. The pundits predicted the nominations of both parties would be locked up by the primaries on Super Tuesday in February. The pundits were wrong about that and about so many other things that most of them gave up predicting. The pre-convention campaign turned out to be one of the longest and most exhausting ever.

The media treated television viewers to a series of debates, alternating between all Republican candidates and all Democratic candidates. Most of the debates were just a series of sound bites that failed to get to important issues. Immigration, border security, treaties, trade, and social issues were conspicuously de-emphasized.

The media were fascinated by what seemed an endless battle between Hillary Clinton and Barack Obama for the Democratic presidential nomination. On May 7, 2008, NBC's Tim Russert called the winner. He declared on MSNBC what the *New York Times* labeled "a devastatingly declarative statement": "We now know who the Democratic nominee's going to be, and no one's going to dispute it." The Democratic Establishment had chosen Barack Obama. Television's political pundits *en masse* immediately shifted hard against Hillary Clinton, virtually demanding that she get out of the race and accept Obama as the party's nominee.

Hillary Clinton and her friends started a chorus of complaints that she had been the victim of sexism. Victimology is a major pillar of feminist ideology. In truth, her once-promising campaign failed because even Democrats suffered from Clinton fatigue and the media had started their love affair with Barack Obama.

The Republican contest was far more complicated and nuanced. Grassroots Republicans were in disarray because they didn't see a candidate who deserved the mantle of Reaganism.

President Bush's disapproval rating rose to 70 percent because of what many considered an unnecessary and badly managed Iraq war, an expanding and ever more expensive government, open borders, free-trade fanaticism that exported millions of well-paid jobs, the sinking value of the dollar, and our growing dependence on foreign goods and foreign loans. Polls reported that 80 percent of Americans said that our nation was going in the wrong direction. All trends indicated that 2008 would be a big year for the Democrats.

Howard Fineman of *Newsweek* looked into his crystal ball and proclaimed the coming crackup of the conservative movement. The *New York Times* published a full-page whine entitled "The Vanishing Establishment: We used to know who called the political shots, but where are the kingmakers now?" The article quoted David Brinkley as observing that "The shift in the sources of funding is profound and probably lasting."

The nomination process of the twenty-first century not only reflected a shift in the sources of political funding but also a shift in geography. Back in 1940, Northeastern and Midwestern states had 251 seats in the U.S. House of Representatives, compared with 184 seats for states in the South and West. By 2008, Southern and Western states had the majority, 252 to 183.

The rapid growth in big government produced about forty thousand registered lobbyists who were hired to seek a share of federal benefits for their clients. The road to riches became K Street, the lobbyists' boulevard. Starting salaries rose to three hundred thousand dollars a year, and retainers of twenty-five thousand to forty thousand dollars a month became typical.

Senator Tom Coburn of Oklahoma described conservatives' dilemma: Republicans are in "paralysis and denial." "Voters are tired of buying a GOP package and finding a big-government liberal agenda inside," he said. We must come to grips with "the triumph of big-government Republicanism and 'compassionate conservatism.'"

The Republican presidential debates started out with ten candidates but none won a majority vote in any of the state primaries. Underneath, the old divisions still existed, as identified by David Limbaugh:

> What we are witnessing is a resurrection of the historical GOP turf war between the Reagan conservatives and the disgruntled Rockefeller moderates. This neo-Rockefeller branch of the GOP apparently believes history has passed traditional conservatism by, that big government is here to stay and not to

be resisted, and that Reagan conservatives should make the best of it and try to
direct government toward conservative
causes. But Reagan conservatives and
libertarians recognize that conservatism
through liberal means is still liberalism.
They strongly reject abandoning their
fealty to fundamental constitutional
restraints on government.

The quintessential neo-Rockefeller candidate in
2008 was the former mayor of New York City Rudy
Giuliani, who had boasted that Nelson Rockefeller
represented "a tradition in the Republican Party I've
worked hard to re-kindle—the Rockefeller, Javits,
Lefkowitz tradition." He started out with a big war
chest, but his brand of pro-gay, pro-abortion, pro-
gun-control Republicanism didn't sell with the voters. and, weighed down by personal scandals, his
campaign collapsed in the Florida primary.

Former Senator Fred Thompson, the hope of many
conservatives, failed to perform on political television as well as he had as a television actor. Reporters
concluded he wasn't particularly interested in being
president, and many speculated that he was really
just a place-holder until the Establishment made its
final decision. Congressmen Duncan Hunter and Tom
Tancredo, Senator Sam Brownback, and Wisconsin

Governor Tommy Thompson each failed to assemble a national campaign. Ron Paul, despite an enthusiastic national following, didn't carry any state.

Former Massachusetts Governor Mitt Romney had plenty of money and a good plan: use his funds to get out the vote in the Iowa caucuses, win in his neighboring state of New Hampshire, and then win in Michigan, where he was born and his father had been governor. But former Arkansas Governor Mike Huckabee, with the backing of the religious right, suddenly rose like a meteor and took Iowa. That opened up New Hampshire for somebody else, and Senator John McCain was ready to step in the gap. In the end, McCain was the only candidate left standing.

McCain made support of the Iraq war his message and his experience as a POW in Vietnam his qualification. Only belatedly did he tackle other issues. He discovered the power of the judicial issue on June 13, 2008, in attacking the Supreme Court decision in the Guantanamo detainee case.[1] When McCain said it was "one of the worst decisions in the history of this country," his audience exploded in applause. Warming to the subject, McCain praised Chief Justice John Roberts for his dissent, calling him the kind of justice he would appoint.

Indeed the assault on our culture by supremacist judges had become an issue that resonated with the voters. The American Bar Association commissioned an Opinion Research poll of Americans' views on the judiciary. People were asked to respond to certain statements by conservative politicians, statements that the ABA considered extreme. The lawyers were shocked to learn that the majority of respondents *agreed* with the supposedly extreme statements. We're fed up with the imperial judiciary, they said. As reported by the *ABA Journal eReport* on October 26, 2005, a majority of Americans agreed that "judicial activism" has reached "a crisis," that judges "ignore traditional morality," that judges are "arrogant, out-of-control and unaccountable," and that judges who ignore voters' values "should be impeached."

Grassroots conservatives accepted their mission to get the Republican Party back on track after eight years of George W. Bush's deviation and globalism. Conservative grassroots Republicanism must be defined and established as different from a Bush party. Conservatives made a great start in doing this by killing George W. Bush's deal to turn over our seaports to a Middle East government agency, Dubai Ports World. Republican grassroots scored a big win by defeating Bush's cooperation with Ted Kennedy to pass an amnesty bill in the Senate.

It gave a positive jolt to John McCain's campaign when he chose Sarah Palin as his running mate. Her campaign for vice president, however, was kept under tight control by McCain's strategists. She complained, "I was not allowed to talk about things [important to grass roots conservatives] because [of] those 'elitists,' those who are the brainiacs in the GOP machine, running John McCain's campaign."

So the voters put their fate in the hands of Barack Obama, a man who said his goal is to "fundamentally transform the United States." Americans didn't anticipate how fundamental that transformation would be.

27

Establishment Strikes Out Again

2012

As the 2012 election approached with Barack Obama and Joe Biden running for reelection, it looked like it should be an easy win for a new team. The majority of Americans told pollsters that our country was going in the wrong direction. As the *Wall Street Journal* observed on February 29, 2012, "Not since Herbert Hoover has a party out of power had such an opportunity to run against everything that troubles the American family—prices, interest rates, unemployment, taxes, or the fear for the future of their old age or the future of their children—than is now presented to the Republican Party. The Republicans, however, haven't figured this out." Widespread opposition to Obamacare should be added to the list of issues that should have been used to discredit Obama.

The Establishment floated a trial balloon for Indiana governor Mitch Daniels, but that hope was dashed by the widespread negative reaction to his comment that presidential candidates should "call a truce on the so-called social issues" and confine themselves to fiscal issues.[1]

After that idea proved a dud, the Establishment chose the next man in line for the presidential nomination, Mitt Romney. He had been runner-up in the previous election. He had a long Republican pedigree, he could boast of significant success in the business world and as managing the Olympic Games, and he had even been elected governor in liberal Massachusetts.

The powers that be were happy that conservatives were divided among several candidates—Rick Santorum, Newt Gingrich, Herman Cain, and Ron Paul—making it easier for the Establishment's choice to lock up the nomination. The huge number of primary debates also gave the Establishment the chance to knock out the candidates they didn't like.

After Mitt Romney's November 2012 defeat, the Republican National Committee issued a ninety-seven-page report that commentators called an "Autopsy." The Republican Party was not really dead as the title implied, but it was bleeding from the Establishment's mistakes, namely, imposing on us a series of losers—Bob Dole, John McCain, and Mitt Romney, all so-called moderates. The highly paid Republican strategists instructed all candidates not to discuss social or moral issues and were so incompetent that they lost nearly all the U.S. Senate races on which they spent three hundred million dollars in television ads (pocketing a handsome percentage of that figure in fees, of course).

Nearly all Republican strategists confidently and publicly predicted that Romney would win the 2012 election. The political writer Jerome Corsi quoted Mitt Romney's chief campaign strategist, Stuart Stevens, as pontificating on the last plane flight of the 2012 campaign that he was confident Mitt Romney would win because "a positive campaign message trumps a good ground game every time." He was wrong. Barack Obama had a first-rate get-out-the-vote game using sophisticated technology, and Republicans didn't have anything remotely comparable. The technology Romney did have crashed on Election Day.

Romney and his paid staff made no effort to reach out to various subgroups such as the Tea Parties, or the Reagan Democrats (who were looking for a leader to stop the hemorrhaging of U.S. jobs to Asia), or the social-issue conservatives. Then Romney insulted the libertarians. Ron Paul claimed 177 duly elected delegates to the 2012 Republican

National Convention in Tampa, but Romney's people refused to allow their votes to be announced during the roll call of states.

The RNC's Autopsy included a lot of chatter about "growth" and "opportunity." Thirty times it brought up the need to be more "inclusive," but that inclusiveness did not extend to those who want to talk about the right to life or traditional marriage. The Autopsy pompously declared, "You have to have candidates who don't make tragic mistakes," but the fatal mistakes were made by the Establishment's own candidates and their strategists. The Establishment has a worse record of picking candidates than the grassroots, who have picked winners such as Ted Cruz, Marco Rubio, Rand Paul, and Mike Lee.

In 2004, a group calling itself the Swift Boat Veterans for Truth launched an independent campaign against Democratic candidate John Kerry's wartime service in Vietnam, turning Kerry's biography into a campaign negative. But two can play at that game, and in 2012 the Democrats turned the tables on the Republicans. They took what Mitt Romney thought was his strongest qualification for leadership, his outstanding business successes, and converted it into a liability. When average voters saw Romney on TV, they didn't see a successful businessman who created jobs; they saw a cost-cutting boss laying off workers.

The liberal pollster Patrick Caddell summarized the Republican problem. "The Republican Party is in the grips of what I call the CLEC—the Consultant, Lobbyist and Establishment Complex," which he defined as a "self-serving interconnected network of individuals interested in preserving their own power far more than in winning elections." Caddell reminded us, "Just follow the money," commenting on the hundreds of millions of dollars this group spent on the losing efforts of most of their so-called "moderate" candidates.

The most insufferable part of the Autopsy's advice is the admonition to embrace comprehensive immigration "reform." Massive evidence collected by Eagle Forum from the leading pollsters proves that endorsing or legislating any form of amnesty will produce votes for Democrats, not Republicans.[2]

Romney never connected with the blocs of grassroots voters he needed to win. And so Barack Obama was reelected to continue, with renewed intensity, his attacks on the U.S. Constitution and on the institution of marriage, his relentless defense of Obamacare, his effort to expunge religion from every public place and event, and his building of the Imperial Presidency.

28

Still Seeking a Choice Not an Echo

2016

*P*olitico reports that closed-door events have already been held for Republican mega-donors to select who will get the big money that went last time to Mitt Romney.

In the *New York Times*, Maureen Dowd warns readers of her column, "Brace yourself for Hillary and Jeb." In the politics section, the *Times* reports how Jeb Bush is so smart, so intellectual, and so well read. We were told that he is a "top-drawer intellect" who maintains twenty-five books on his Kindle, including George Gilder's *Knowledge and Power*. The *Times* also reported that Jeb takes vacations called "think week" where the agenda is the analysis of political proposals.

Do you get the message that the media buildup for Jeb Bush has begun and that the 2016 Republican

National Convention may nominate another Establishment loser, the next one in line? But it doesn't have to be. Some of us remember Everett Dirksen's famous speech at the 1952 Republican convention, when he publicly taunted the kingmakers, "We followed you before and you led us down the path to defeat."

No, the 2016 nomination for president is not locked up yet. Jeb Bush has many fatal liabilities, such as the Bush name and his vehement support of the Common Core takeover of our schools. If conservatives want to nominate a real conservative, they must get busy now.

Do conservatives have a future? Can we hope again to offer the American people a choice not an echo—a presidential candidate who is an authentic conservative and who responds to the grassroots instead of to the kingmakers?

We've done it before—we can do it again. We did it in 1964 when we overcame the Rockefeller machine and nominated Barry Goldwater. We did it again in 1980 when we defeated the Establishment choice, George H. W. Bush, and nominated and elected Ronald Reagan, the greatest president of the twentieth century.

We've survived bouts of adversity like Watergate and congressional election defeats and gone on to accomplish great things for our country. Let's remember—when the fishermen Apostles complained to Jesus that they were hungry and the fish weren't biting, Jesus told them, "Let down your nets for the catch," and they caught plenty of fish. There are millions of conservatives who believe in America; it's up to us to find them and get them to vote and to participate in our political process so we can preserve this great country that God has blessed so richly.

Conservatives today are depressed. They feel we've been repeatedly stuck with Big Government Republicans who have increased spending, tried to federalize education, and turned out to be New World Order globalists.

Obama has provoked cries of "Imperial Presidency" from both ends of the political spectrum as he violates the constitutional limits on his power. Obama bragged, "We are not just going to be waiting for legislation. I have a pen and I've got a phone. And I can use that pen to sign executive orders and take executive actions." Americans have many other problems with Obama. He lied to us: "If you like your health insurance, you can keep it." He tries to banish mention of God from every public event and place; he quotes the Declaration of Independence while omitting the word Creator.

Grassroots conservatives should focus on the following key issues:

- *Bringing supremacist judges under control and restoring Americans' self-rule.* We must reject rule by robed masters who believe the U.S. Constitution is a "living" document which they can reinterpret according to their own preferences and "evolving standards." Judges cannot be allowed to declare unconstitutional the Pledge of Allegiance, the Ten Commandments, the Boy Scout oath, the traditional definition of marriage, parents' rights in public schools, or a cross to honor the dead.

- *American sovereignty.* We must defeat all United Nations treaties that cut away some of our sovereignty, such as the Law of the Sea Treaty, which Ronald Reagan rejected long ago. That treaty would give control of all the oceans and the riches at the bottom of the sea to a United Nations organization, create a world court to decide disputes, and grant power to impose taxes. We must defeat all plans for a North American Union modeled on the European Union, which would be a fatal blow to U.S.

independence. "Economic integration" and "labor mobility"—meaning open borders for cheap labor—are already being foisted upon us through the government's refusal to enforce the laws against the entry and the hiring of illegal aliens and the linguistic apartheid misleadingly called bilingual education. Our schools must not teach our youngsters to become "citizens of the world" or allow them to grow up without speaking English.

- *Right to life.* The pro-life plank in the Republican platform testifies that the Republican Party has been officially pro-life ever since *Roe v. Wade.* The pro-life constituency is essential to conservative election victories.

- *Marriage.* The passage of marriage amendments in thirty-three states, plus the passage by Congress of the Defense of Marriage Act, confirms that the majority of Americans support the traditional definition of marriage: the union of one man and one woman. We cannot permit supremacist judges to overturn the definition of marriage as recognized in our law and culture for millennia. If we are to remain a self-governing people, we must not allow what Abraham Lincoln called "that eminent tribunal" to redefine our fundamental social norms and policies. Conservatives should affirm the importance of marriage and the legal norm that children be raised by their own married mother and father, not only as a moral objective but also as an economic and political good. We must challenge and repeal the legislative and financial incentives for divorce and illegitimacy that the feminist movement has built into welfare spending.

- *Parents' right to direct the raising and education of their own children*. Parents, not the "village" or judges, must make decisions regarding what is in "the best interest of the child."
- *Protection of American workers*. We must terminate or renegotiate the trade agreements that pretend to promote free trade but actually are a cover for out-sourcing good American jobs, in-sourcing foreigners to take jobs away from Americans, and

allowing foreign countries to discriminate against U.S. products. We must reject the proposed changes in our patent law that benefit foreign countries at the expense of American inventors and benefit multinationals at the expense of small business and inventors.

- *Immigration and border security.* Amnesty for illegal aliens—even incremental amnesty that goes by the name of "comprehensive" immigration reform—must be rejected. Americans must demand border security, a double fence, more border guards, compulsory use of E-Verify, the tracking of visitors' visas, local police cooperation with federal immigration authority, and an end to the practice of granting automatic citizenship to "anchor babies." The billions of dollars spent on the so-called war against drugs must be recognized as a sham so long as most illegal drugs are allowed to come across our southern border.

It's up to grassroots Americans to rebuild the conservative movement and take back the Republican

Party from the RINOs (as we did so successfully in 1964 and 1980).

Strong words about the need for grassroots action have come even from an Establishment Republican, the former chairman of the Republican National Committee and governor of Mississippi, Haley Barbour. He told the RNC at its January 2008 winter meeting, "We've become a top-down party.... We have to become a bottom-up party again."

Ronald Reagan said that God's hand is on America. We have inherited a wonderful land of liberty and prosperity. It's our duty to safeguard our magnificent heritage. We must avail ourselves of the procedures provided in the U.S. Constitution and the mechanisms of self-government and party politics. Our country is in peril, and saving America is up to grassroots Americans.

The Reagan model teaches that authentic conservatism and traditional-values coalitions are the road to political victory. Conservative Republicans don't have to settle for a liberal or a moderate masquerading as a conservative because conservatives have the majority to demand candidates with the right stuff. Conservatives should learn how to identify and reject me-too and RINO candidates.

Americans are seeking leaders who support a pro-American foreign policy and who will wage forceful opposition to any global or North American "web" of institutions, United Nations orders, treaties, and trade agreements that subsidize or encourage the process of replacing our once-prosperous middle class with cheap labor from foreign countries.

Americans are seeking leaders to support conservative domestic policies including real tax cuts and a major reduction in Big Government. Americans are seeking leaders who will mount principled opposition to the federal government's efforts to control classroom curricula and health care and to monitor the daily lives of law-abiding citizens. More than 80 percent of Americans want English legislated as our official language because they know that a common tongue is essential to living our national motto, *e pluribus unum*.

Americans are seeking leaders who defend the Creator-endowed rights of every individual to life and liberty and the authority of both parents (even if divorced) over the care and upbringing of their own children. Americans want leaders who will speak out against a centrally mandated school curriculum, appropriations that incentivize bad conduct, and anti-parent court decisions.

Americans want presidential and congressional leaders who truly offer a choice not an echo of past policies. It's time for all conservatives and grassrooters to engage in the political battle and make sure we have candidates we can support.

The kingmakers are playing for high stakes—control of federal spending—and they do not intend to lose. Americans must learn the significance of Patrick Henry's famous lines from 1775: "I have but one lamp by which my feet are guided, and that is the lamp of experience. I know of no way of judging the future but by the past."

That's the challenge for grassroots conservatives. In the words of our great first president, George Washington, "Let us raise a standard to which the wise and honest can repair. The event is in the hand of God."

About the Author

The quadrennial Republican National Conventions have been one of Phyllis Schlafly's lifetime hobbies ever since she attended the 1952 convention in Chicago and observed how crooked and mysterious they can be. When Republican grassroots were trying to nominate Barry Goldwater for president in the early 1960s, she determined that convention delegates should be accurately informed about the inside story of how American presidents are chosen. She self-published *A Choice Not An Echo* in 1964 and sold three million copies out of her garage—a publishing sensation. That book converted people and became a major force in starting the conservative movement.

Mrs. Schlafly has continued to monitor Republican National Conventions and has played an active role in every convention from 1952 through 2012, serving as an elected delegate nine times (1956, 1964, 1968, 1984, 1988, 1992, 1996, 2004, and 2012) and an elected alternate delegate four times (1960, 1980, 2000, and 2008). She has served several times on the platform committee, most recently in 2012. She is credited with making sure that the Republican platform has endorsed the right to life ever since *Roe v. Wade*, has opposed the fraudulent Equal Rights Amendment in the platform ever since 1980, and has consistently endorsed U.S. military superiority.

Mrs. Schlafly received her B.A. from Washington University, her M.A. from Harvard University, her J.D. from Washington University Law School, and an honorary doctorate of humane letters from Washington University. More information about Mrs. Schlafly can be found at www.eagleforum.org, including a list of the twenty books she has written on subjects as varied as the strategic balance, the judiciary, school curriculum, politics, and feminism. She is the mother of six grown children.

Notes

Chapter 2: Who's Looney Now?

1. Associated Press Dispatch from Moscow, January 17, 1964.
2. *U.S. News and World Report*, December 27, 1957, 32.
3. *Washington Post*, July 6, 1960.
4. Associated Press Dispatch.
5. Ibid.
6. Released September 1961, Government Printing Office, Washington, D.C.
7. *Congressional Record*, June 19, 1962, 9966–8.
8. Special Report on the Phoenix Study, U.S.A. vol. 10, nos. 24, 25, and 26.
9. *U.S. News and World Report*, January 27, 1964, 31.
10. Victor Riesel Column, January 20, 1964.
11. Associated Press Dispatch, January 17, 1964.
12. *New York Journal American*, March 2–5, 1964.

13. Allen-Scott Report, March 6, 1964.

14. *U.S. News and World Report,* June 25, 1954, 79–80;
     also June 11, 1954, 82ff.

15. *Doubleday and Co. v. New York,* 335 U.S. 848, Octo-
     ber 25, 1948.

16. Edmund Wilson, *The Cold War and the Income Tax,*
     115.

17. United Press Dispatch, August 30, 1963.

18. Marguerite Higgins, "Our Country's Inglorious Role
     in the Final Days of the Diem Regime," *Human
     Events* (March 7, 1964): 8–9.

19. Allen-Scott Report, February 21, 1964.

Chapter 3: Republicans Can't Lose—Unless

1. James L. Wick, *How Not to Run for President* (New
    York: Vantage Press, Inc., 1952), 19–24.

2. Congressional Record, May 31, 1955, A3761.

Chapter 4: The Smoke-Filled Room

1. Quoted in *One Man: Wendell Willkie* by C. Nelson
    Sparks (New York: Rayner, 1943), 5–7.

2. Arthur M. Schlesinger Jr., *The Politics of Upheaval*
    (Boston: Houghton Mifflin Co., 1960), 539.

3. Ibid, 533.

Chapter 5: The Advertising Agent's Holiday: 1940

1. Joseph Barnes, *Willkie* (New York: Simon and
    Schuster, 1952), 152.

2.   Donald Bruce Jackson, *The Republican Party and Wendell Willkie* (Urbana: University of Illinois Press, 1960), 50.

3.   Ibid, 64–65.

4.   Congressional Record, June 19, 1940, 12960.

5.   Barnes, 178.

6.   Sparks, 18.

7.   Ibid., 20.

8.   U.S. Senate Foreign Relations Committee Hearings, February 11, 1941.

Chapter 6: The Pollsters and the Hoaxers: 1944

1.   Ralph de Toledano, *The Winning Side* (New York: G. P. Putnam's Sons, 1963), 84.

Chapter 7: Snatching Defeat from the Jaws of Victory: 1948

1.   Jules Abels, *Out of the Jaws of Victory* (New York: Henry Holt and Company, 1959), 63.

2.   Wick, chapter 7.

3.   *Roll Call*, October 26, 1960.

Chapter 8: The Big Steal: 1952

1.   *National Review,* October 5, 1957, 295.

2.   Speech at University of Pennsylvania, April 18, 1952.

3.   July 5, 1952.

4.	Edwin A. Roberts Jr., *Elections 1964*, Newsbook, the *National Observer* (Silver Spring, Maryland, 1964), 68.

5.	Idem.

6.	*Chicago Tribune*, July 11, 1952.

7.	*New York Times*, November 25, 1959, 14.

8.	*American Bar Journal*, February 1958, 113–114, 192.

Chapter 9: Here Comes That Man Again: 1956

1.	*New York Times*, July 24 and 31, 1956.

2.	Walter Trohan, "The Stassen-Clay Plot That Failed," *Human Events* (October 13, 1961): 679.

Chapter 10: Surrender in Manhattan: 1960

1.	*New York Times*, July 25, 1960.

2.	*East St. Louis Journal*, July 27, 1960.

3.	*Newsweek*, March 23, 1964, 24–25.

4.	*Virginian-Pilot*, April 28, 1963, A-13.

Chapter 12: Anybody but Goldwater

1.	"Anatomy of the Goldwater Boom," by Tom Wicker, *New York Times Magazine*, August 11, 1963.

2.	*Human Events*, August 3, 1963, 10.

3.	Jules Witcover, "The Making of a Presidential Candidate," *St. Louis Globe-Democrat*, February 1–2, 1964; GOP's Political Pros Undecided as Amateurs Spotlight Governor Scranton," by Raymond P. Brandt, *St. Louis Post-Dispatch*, February 8, 1964;

"GOP Old Pros Take Good Look at Scranton," by Rowland Evans and Robert Novak, *St. Louis Post-Dispatch*, January 21, 1964.

4.   Petition distributed at Lincoln Day gathering of Missouri Republicans, Sheraton-Jefferson Hotel, St. Louis, Missouri, February 15, 1964.

5.   *St. Louis Globe-Democrat,* op. cit.

Chapter 13: Victory for the Grassroots: 1964

1.   William S. White, *Los Angeles Times*, July 17, 1964.

2.   *Chicago Tribune,* May 29, 1964.

3.   *San Francisco Examiner,* July 18, 1964.

4.   *St. Louis Globe-Democrat*, May 23, 1964.

Chapter 14: Who Are the Secret Kingmakers?

1.   "Who Are They," U.S. House Committee on Un-American Activities, October 17, 1957.

2.   Associated Press Dispatch, March 26, 1964.

3.   "A World Effectively Controlled by the UN," ARPA-IDA Study Memo No. 7, March 10, 1962, Dept. of State Contract SCC 28270, February 24, 1961.

Chapter 15: The Swing to the Right: 1968

1.   *New York Times*, May 30, 1969.

2.   Syndicated column, December 2, 1968.

3.   *Battle Line,* February 1970.

Chapter 16: Betrayal at the Top: 1972

1. The SALT I Agreement allowed the Soviets 1,618 intercontinental ballistic missiles to our 1,054, allowed the Russians sixty-two submarines for launching ballistic missiles to our forty-four, allowed the Russians 950 ballistic missile launchers on submarines to our 710, and allowed the Russians a missile throw-weight advantage of at least four-to-one. Kissinger's role in the SALT I agreements is reported in detail in *Kissinger on the Couch* by Phyllis Schlafly and Rear Admiral Chester Ward, USN (Ret.) (New Rochelle, N.Y.: Arlington House, 1975).

2. *With No Apologies: The Personal and Political Memoirs of United States Senator Barry M. Goldwater* (New York: William Morrow & Co., 1979), 11.

3. CBS Spectrum Radio Broadcast, February 4, 1974.

Chapter 17: The Accidental President: 1974

1. One day, while I was visiting in the Chicago office of the CEO of a large insurance company, James S. Kemper, the phone rang with a call from his good friend, the governor of Michigan. The two often cooperated in donating to Republican congressional candidates. The governor requested a substantial donation to a Michigan candidate named Gerald Ford. Kemper said, "Sure, I'll send him a check. Is he a good guy?" The Michigan governor

responded, "Yes, he's a good man. Of course, I would never want to see him in any really big job."

2. Phyllis Schlafly, "Plotting to Rewrite the Constitution," Copley News Service, January 8, 1987.

Chapter 18: Climbing Up the Hill: 1976

1. Henry Kissinger's manipulation of Gerald Ford's relationship with the Soviet Union is described in *Ambush at Vladivostok* by Phyllis Schlafly and Rear Adm. Chester Ward, USN (Ret.) (Alton, Ill.: Pere Marquette Press, 1976).

2. Zbigniew Brzezinski, *Between Two Ages: America's Role in the Technetronic Era* (New York: Viking, 1970), 28, 104.

3. Ibid., 99.

4. Goldwater, *With No Apologies*, 285.

5. Ibid., 284.

Chapter 19: Victory for Conservatives: 1980

1. John Anderson showed his true colors years later when he became the president of the United World Federalists. On Chris Matthews's CNBC television show, *Hardball*, October 16, 1998, Anderson revealed that he voted for Walter Mondale in 1984, Michael Dukakis in 1988, Bill Clinton in 1992, and in 1996 cast a write-in vote for Ralph Nader because Clinton was "too conservative."

2.   After a two-and-a-half-year lawsuit, the U.S. District Court ruled on December 23, 1981, in *Idaho v. Freeman* that the ERA time extension was unconstitutional. When the case was appealed to the U.S. Supreme Court, it was dismissed as "moot" on October 4, 1982. The Supreme Court cited as controlling the memorandum of the U.S. Administrator of General Services, who had argued that "the Amendment has failed of adoption no matter what the resolution of the legal issues presented here" about the constitutionality of the extension. Thus, the Supreme Court held, and all parties agreed, that ERA was dead whether ERA expired on March 22, 1979, or on June 30, 1982.

Chapter 20: Defining Conservatism In Dallas: 1984

1.   For an analysis of the importance of Reykjavík, see Charles Krauthammer, "Arms Control: The End of an Illusion," *Weekly Standard*, November 1, 1999.

Chapter 21: Bidin' My Time: 1988

1.   Robert James Bidinotto, "Getting Away With Murder," *Reader's Digest*, July 1988.

Chapter 22: The Man Who Didn't Learn: 1992

1. New York: Macmillan Co., 1996. For a brief summary of the highlights of this lengthy book, see the *Phyllis Schlafly Report*, April 1971.

2. Three of President John F. Kennedy's most influential advisers were Rhodes scholars and ardent anglophiles: Dean Rusk, Walt W. Rostow, and Senator J. William Fulbright. President Clinton appointed a record number of Rhodes scholars, including Secretary of Labor Robert Reich; his special adviser on Russia and number-two man in the State Department, Strobe Talbott; the director of Central Intelligence, James Woolsey; his communications director, George Stephanopoulos; Secretary of the Navy Richard Danzig; his senior advisor for policy development (and the author of Clinton's health care and education proposals), Ira Magaziner; the director of the National Economic Council, Bonnie St. John Deane; the director of the Office of Management and Budget, Franklin Raines, Deputy Under Secretary of Defense for Policy Walter Slocombe; the supreme commander of NATO, Wesley Clark (who directed the bombing of Yugoslavia); and his impeachment defense attorney, David Kendall. For a more complete list, see Dennis Laurence Cuddy, *Secret Records Revealed* (Oklahoma City, Hearthstone Publishing Ltd., 1999), especially pages 152–53.

Chapter 23: The Dole Debacle: 1996

1. Colin Powell with Joseph Persico, *My American Journey* (New York: Random House, 1995).

2. *New York Times*, October 3, 1995. Maybe Powell picked up his affinity for Nelson Rockefeller from Powell's writer, Joseph Persico, who had previously been a speechwriter for Rockefeller.

3. Powell's remark wasn't out of character. In his autobiography, *My American Journey*, he wrote, "I am troubled by the political passion of those on the extreme right who seem to claim divine wisdom on political as well as spiritual matters" (608).

4. *Chicago Sun-Times*, October 25, 1995. Among other perceptive press pieces that caused bumps in Powellmania were "Noncandidate Powell Stirs Waves on Republican Right," *New York Times*, October 3, 1995, 1, and George Will's syndicated column, "Seeking Answers to Powell's Inconsistencies," October 30, 1995.

5. Strobe Talbot, "The Birth of the Global Nation," *Time*, July 20, 1992.

Chapter 24: Follow the Big Money: 2000

1. ABC *This Week*, November 28, 1999.

Chapter 25: Seeking A New World Order: 2004

1. Robert Novak, "Dictated by Bush," August 26, 2004.

2. *New York Times*, July 7, 2004.

3.   Matthew Latimer, *Speech-less: Tales of a White House Survivor* (New York: Crown, 2009).

Chapter 26: Fundamentally Transforming America: 2008

1.   *Boumediene v. Bush*, 553 U.S. 723.

Chapter 27: Establishment Strikes Out Again: 2012

1.   Andrew Ferguson, "Ride Along with Mitch," *Weekly Standard*, June 14, 2010.
2.   Eagle Forum, *How Mass (Legal) Immigration Dooms a Conservative Republican Party* (2014).

Index